Win At Life
Tips & Skills for Tackling Life From Unlikely Places
By Fuad A. Kamal

Book Version: 0.92 B

Table of Contents

This book is dedicated to my loving mom from whom I learnt so much.

Introduction

Want to learn tips and skills for doing well at life? Well let's dive in...

The book is divided into two sections. The first section identifies key skills important for success in life. The second section looks at how one might apply these skills to achieve goals that one has identified as being important. This distinction is important since simply learning skills is only part of the equation for success. Much like the sailor who learns to optimize the sails to the prevailing winds, if the sailor is sailing in the completely wrong direction, those wonderful skills will only lead one far away from happiness and fulfillment. Thus, the second part of the book concludes with some reflections about the direction of the journey.

Okay enough about that.

What exciting things await me?

In the very short time it takes to finish this book, you will get exposed to fascinating stories, studies, and anecdotes from an eclectic assortment of sources including:

» mathematics
» history
» fables
» language

- » economics
- » psychology
- » biology
- » business
- » artificial intelligence
- » racing
- » politics

Yet, somehow in the process, we will endeavor to extract some valuable, personal lessons. Wondering how? Read on.

To pique your curiosity, here are some interesting points that will be explored as you turn the pages of this book:

- » Can it ever help to be lazy?
- » How can one energize creativity?
- » How to beat the smartest person in the room?
- » Do dogs care about fairness?
- » Does a rat have empathy?
- » How can you increase your odds of living longer?
- » Why very bright minds spend billions of dollars in fields littered with failure?
- » Would you like to do things without effort?
- » A trick to help you negotiate a better salary?
- » What do athletes know about failure?
- » What's the easiest way to be wealthy?
- » Is there an easier way to exercise?

» What can an economist who died over a hundred years ago teach you about productivity today?

Interested now?

BOOK ROADMAP

The book launches with an exploration of key qualities or traits. These are the "super ingredients" of a successful life. After discussing the "how" of success, we move onto the question of "what is success?" It's a basic reality check to make sure that you are utilizing your newfound skills to build a fuller, happier life for yourself. We reflect on your pathways to happiness. Finally, we touch on two core human qualities: compassion and justice, since they are fundamental to this experience called life.

Let us now explore the first super-ingredient for success, which is the subject of the next chapter.

Tip: Do you want a quicker, lighter read the first time you read this book? Then skip reading the parts marked "optional."

Section I: Skills

Chapter 1
Drive

Why do we care about drive?

Because it is one of the "super-ingredients" to being successful in your dreams–in your life. As such, it is worthwhile exploring what "drive" is. It is the topic of this chapter.

What is the formula for drive?

Drive = $I + B + P^2 + R$

(Don't worry, it's not a complicated formula.)

PASSION

> "Dreams are the touchstones of our character." Henry David Thoreau

> "If you take any activity, any art, any discipline, any skill–take it and push it as far as it will go; push it beyond where it has ever been before; push it to the wildest edges of edges; then you force it into the realm of magic." Tom Robbins

Drive is the secret ingredient to succeeding where others fail. The essence of drive is passion and dreams. Its fuel is persistence. Its shock absorbers are resilience. Its calling card is boldness and initiative in the face of obstacles.

Drive = (I)nitiative + (B)elief + (P)assion * (P)ersistence + (R)esilience

During the rest of this chapter you will be closely exploring each of these components, deriving insights from a variety of disciplines.

BOLDNESS & INITIATIVE

"Fortune favors the Bold" Latin proverb

Are boldness and initiative really that important in life?

To bring this point home let us look at something so pervasive and common that it permeates pretty much everyone's human experience. Let see how big an impact it can have on a core human endeavor that is central to human existence. If we can show it to have an important impact there, the basic premise can easily be extended elsewhere.

What are we talking about here? Partner selection. Pervasive. Central.

In order to set the background for this discussion, let us begin with an assumption. Assume that there are only five boys and five girls in the world. Yeah, I know, small world.

Consider this scenario/selection process:

In order to select their spouses the boys approach the girls *in the order of their interest*. Thus a boy will approach the girl he is *most* interested in *first*. If more than one boy approaches a girl she will select between them. The rejected boys will then approach their second choices. The cycle will repeat until all the boys and girls are paired off.

That's the end of selections. Everyone goes off into the sunset. The world is saved, and they all lived happily ever after.

Sure, why not? But let's dissect the matching process and analyze how well the boys did relative to the girls. If you look carefully (actually, very carefully), the boys fared "better" than the girls. Why? Intrigued? Read on...

Well, let's assume the most popular girl got two interested boys in the first round. When she makes her first decision she is only selecting between TWO boys. However, all the boys are signaling their interest to their first choice amongst all FIVE girls in their first decision. *In essence, the boys are striving for their best choice, whereas the girls are striving for their least bad choice!*

The boys are exchanging a slightly better outcome in exchange for their willingness to deal with rejection. The group that took the initiative (and risked rejection/humiliation) fared much better!

This logic extends far beyond the romantic arena. For example, it is usually far better for you to approach companies for jobs than to have them approach you.

Moral of the story: Take the initiative![1] It pays!

THE POWER OF BELIEVING AND COMMITTING

When someone truly, really believes in something, his/her actions can be transformative. When someone really believes and commits to something, a hidden reservoir of strength is released.

---

1   If you are interested in this check out Hannah Fry's entertaining exploration of the Gale-Shapley matching algorithm (the above is based on that), optimal stopping theory, and others in her "Mathematics of Love" book.

Skeptical?

Let us examine two parallel historical incidents almost a thousand years apart. Both speak about the power of commitment. Both are major turning points in history. Both resulted in enormous victories against all odds. Both engaged in one identical critical act.

» In 711, Tariq ibn Ziyad landed in Gibraltar from North Africa at the head of a small force. He went on to conquer Hispania (Spain).

» In 1519, Hernán Cortés (a Spanish conquistador) landed in the Mexican coast at Yucatan at the head of a very small force. He then went on to conquer the Aztec Empire (Mexico).

What did they both have in common? Soon after arrival, both men ordered the destruction of their ships. By this simple act, their men had crossed the point of no return. There simply was no retreat. They had committed in the strongest way possible. They simply had no choice but to succeed against all odds.

Commitment is not just a historical fact. For example, it is relevant in business today. Marketer Seth Godin in his 2014 book Tribes notes, "In a battle between two ideas, the best one doesn't necessarily win. No, the idea that wins is the one with the most fearless heretic behind it."

Commitment can unleash powerful forces.

(Note: Commitment is powerful, so make sure you believe in the right things first.)

RESILIENCE

Resilience is a key component of drive–a super ingredient for success. So what can one do to build resilience? Let's go a little offbeat for this one. Let's make it interesting. How about an example dealing with the internet? After all, resilience is a critical issue facing internet companies.

Companies face the problem of trying to present a seamless, consistent user experience to their customers, while in the background dealing with equipment that can degrade, crash, and malfunction. While engineers can set up the processes, protocols, and methods for automatically detecting and healing problems, there are few things that work as well as *rehearsing resilience.*

Netflix has blogged on its ability to deliberately affect "chaos" to its own systems to check that its processes and procedures are resilient and effective in quickly recovering from any problems. Its "Simian Army" can seed (controlled) chaos by terminating instances (e.g. computers) or slowing matters to a snail's pace at selected systems in order to test for resiliency. Thus, it can continuously check its responsive systems to ensure that its network is actually resilient and responsive.[2]

Moral: Analyze your resilience "systems." Mentally simulate various possible scenarios. Find weak spots. Fix them. Like any muscle, resilience can get stronger. Also don't forget humor - it too can be a great resilience booster.

---

[2]   http://techblog.netflix.com/2011/07/netflix-simian-army.html

PERSISTENCE

> "Genius is one percent inspiration and ninety-nine percent perspiration." Thomas A. Edison

> "Anyone who thinks sitting in church can make you a Christian must also think that sitting in a garage can make you a car." Garrison Keillor

> "Seventy percent of success in life is showing up." Woody Allen

> "The brick walls are there for a reason. The brick walls are not there to keep us out. The brick walls are there to give us a chance to show how badly we want something. Because the brick walls are there to stop the people who don't want it badly enough. They're there to stop the other people." Randy Pausch, The Last Lecture

Next ,we will explore persistence across several different areas, including psychology, publishing, and history.

PSYCHOLOGY RESEARCH

Persistence is important. "Practice, practice, practice" as the mantra goes. In a concept popularized by Malcolm Gladwell in his book "Outliers," and based on Anders Ericsson's research, the "10,000 hour rule" suggests that acquiring sufficient mastery over a skill might take 10,000 hours.

So working at 20 hours/week at a skill would translate into roughly 10 years of practice to develop one's expertise. So persevere if you really want to become an expert at something! It takes time.

Dr Seuss – Case

Consider the case of the famous children's book author Dr. Seuss. Did you know that his first book was rejected by between 20 to 43 publishers? It is said that he was so discouraged that he almost burnt his book. Apparently, serendipity intervened, and a chance encounter eventually led to the publication. He then went on to become a best-selling children's author.

Moral of the story: Don't give up!

Case study – History

"Big shots are only little shots who keep shooting."
Christopher Morley

Persistence/Resilience

The Empire that Almost Never Was

Born under the thumb of foreign overlords, sacked, beaten, and then defeated, these peoples then became entangled in an epic battle with an audacious rival. During at least one engagement, they managed to lose almost their entire navy, and suffered humiliating, devastating, soul-shattering losses at land.

One might rightfully wonder if a "loser" nation like this could even survive?

You may be surprised to hear we are talking about the unlikely historical beginnings of the Romans – one of the greatest powers of the ancient world.

To put it in perspective, here is a short timeline of those events:

753 BCE Establishment of Rome by the Tiber River

500 BCE Rome ruled by foreign Etruscan kings (e.g., Northern Italy)

390 BCE Rome sacked by a Celtic invasion from Gaul (e.g., France)

321 BCE Rome beaten at Battle of Caudine Forks by Samnites (e.g., Southern Italy)

280s BCE General Pryrrhus of Epirus (e.g. Greece/Albania) defeated the Roman Republic in southern Italy by destroying two Roman armies.

264 BCE to 146 BCE Punic wars were between Rome and arch-rival Carthage (part of North Africa/Spain and centered on modern-day Tunisia).

The wars between Rome and Carthage, referred to as the Punic Wars by historians, were one of the epic conflicts of the ancient world.

For a variety of reasons, Rome found itself embroiled in a conflict with Carthage. The conflict began with the First Punic War. There was one problem for the Romans. The conflict was centered on the Mediterranean, and Rome, unlike Carthage — an established naval power, did not have a fleet. Rome was primarily a land power.

So what did the Romans do? Naturally, they built an entire fleet! Seizing upon a grounded Carthaginian quinquereme (i.e. warship) they reverse engineered its design. However they did not stop there; they modified the design. Next, they launched a wildly ambitious, industrial scale project to build an entire navy practically overnight. I guess one can say they had spunk! In record time, the Romans had a navy.

However this Roman spirit was soon tested. The Romans lost the bulk of their naval fleet not once but *twice*: in 255 BCE (off Camarina, Sicily) and in 253 BCE (off Libya) in storms. In 255 BCE, the Roman fleet was sent to evacuate Roman Consul Regulus' forces, which were fleeing from Carthage, and was destroyed in a storm. In one of the worst naval disasters in history, around 90,000 men were lost. In 253 BCE, the rebuilt Roman fleet hit another storm off Libya, and around 150 ships were lost. Nor was this the end of Rome's problems. Huge numbers of ships in their fleets were destroyed in at least two other encounters. In one case, Roman consul Publius Claudius Pulcher lost ninety ships near the Sicilian coast. In another, a storm in eastern Sicily devastated a Roman fleet of over hundred ships.

Amazingly, despite it all, the Romans *doggedly persevered* and pulled ahead of Carthage in the First Punic War.

The Second Punic War was especially colorful since it involved one of history most famous generals – Carthaginian general Hannibal. Yes, the same one who executed one of the ancient world's most mind boggling and dramatic military maneuvers ever by marching war elephants(!) across one of Europe's highest mountain ranges, i.e., the Alps, into Italy.

Hannibal's spectacular Italian entry resulted in a resounding series of defeats for the Romans. They were defeated at Ticinus, Trebia, and Trasimene. In 217 BCE, Lake Trasimene was an especially potent defeat where the Romans were caught in a surprise ambush

19

by the lake as Hannibal's hidden troops descended from the surrounding hills.

However, it is at the famous Battle of Cannae (216 BCE) that Rome suffered one of its worst military disasters ever. Two armies, compromising around 70,000 Romans, were simply annihilated by Hannibal.

Yet, despite all this, Rome went on to defeat Carthage and became one of the most powerful empires in human history. There are a number of explanations[3] for this phenomenon, but one simply cannot discount the one overarching quality: perseverance, without which nothing would have been possible. *The Romans simply never gave up.*

These stories are not uncommon for important human events in history. Several major empires were built from the ashes of failure. Let us visit another major population center of the world, i.e., South Asia. Here are the (very abbreviated) stories of two rulers of India who suffered major reversals before their ascent.

BABUR

He inherited the throne of Fergana when he was twelve and conquered Samarkand by age fourteen. Shortly afterward, he lost them both. He was then defeated in 1501 by Muhammad Shaybani of the Uzbeks

---

3   During Rome's early conquest of Italy, it had taken the unusual (for the ancient world) step of conferring varying degrees of citizenship on conquered peoples (instead of killing, enslaving, etc.). This allowed Rome to massively expand its relatively loyal manpower reserves for its troops. It also converted its army to a more professional footing. The army was also very adaptable (for example, an iconic Roman sword was actually adopted from the enemy hill tribes of Spain). Finally, it appears that wealthy Romans were more consistently committed and enthusiastic in fielding troops and supplies for the war than their Carthaginian counterparts.

when he tried to reclaim Samarkind. He then lived in poverty and exile with his uncle in Tashkent.

He began his upswing by conquering Kabul but was driven out in a revolt by his generals. He later regained Kabul and then Samarkand, along with Bokhara, before losing Samarkand and Bokhara to the Uzbeks

Despite it all, he persisted and went on to found the famous Mughal dynasty in India.

MUHAMMAD OF GHOR (E.G. AFGHANISTAN)

His first encounter in 1178 with an Indian ruler, Queen Naikidevi, resulted in a defeat and retreat at the battle of Kayadara (Gujarat).

More critically and more ominously, in the first battle of Tarain in 1191, he was wounded in personal combat with Prithviraj's brother, Govind Tai. He was very lucky to be able to retreat his forces despite being injured.

Despite it all, he persisted and went on to become an important ruler in India.

Both individuals had a major effect on the course of human history. This was so much so that their (eventually successful) actions marked important turning points in human history.

SUMMARY

Drive = (I)nitiative + (B)elief + (P)assion * (P)ersistence + (R)esilience

"If one advances confidently in the direction of his dreams, and endeavors to live the life which he has imagined, he will meet with a success unexpected in common hours." Henry David Thoreau

Learn to harness drive to propel yourself into success in life.

Chapter 2
Imagination: "Thinking Outside the Box"

"It's kind of fun to do the impossible." Walt Disney

THE NATURE OF LUCK

Can you become lucky?

Some people seem to have all the luck. "If only I had that much luck, I would do great too", you say. Well, what if you could increase your "luck"? or Create your own "luck?"

Well there is a great saying that goes:

"Luck is what happens when preparation meets opportunity." Seneca the Younger

Smart people realize that "luck" can be "manipulated."

CASE (MEDICAL)

Consider Dr. Alexander Fleming, the discoverer of penicillin and one of the greatest scientists of the modern era. Antibiotics are one of the great breakthroughs in modern medicine. However, did you know that the discovery of penicillin was an accident? Apparently, Dr. Fleming returned from vacation to find one of his petri dishes containing staphylococcus aureus colonies had been contaminated.

Instead of ignoring the contaminated sample, Fleming chose to put the petri dish under a microscope.

23

What he found next turned out to become one of the turning points of medical history. The microscope revealed that while the bacteria grew throughout the dish, there was one clear distinctive spot where it did not grow. That part of the dish had been contaminated by the intrusion of a rare mold–penicillium notatum. Apparently, something in the mold was suppressing the bacteria! This was the origin of how antibiotics – one of medicine's revolutionary breakthroughs – were discovered.

Note: The skeptic may point out it was "dumb luck." However, this completely misses key points. For example, many people would have simply discarded the "contaminated" dishes. Fleming's key genius was his *curiosity*. While a lesser person may have simply discarded the contaminated sample, Fleming's naturally curious mind and rigorous scientific training instead led him to examine the evidence further. In doing so, he essentially created, or multiplied, his own "luck" and made medical history. Preparation + opportunity = luck.

CASES (BUSINESS)

The importance of curiosity and imagination goes far beyond the medical domain. There are many stories of fortunes being made because of bold, innovative thinking "outside the box." One can, for example, look at the stories of some of America's richest men.

Consider the case of Rockefeller. Did you know that his oil (kerosene) was originally sold to light the homes in the U.S. (American houses had previously used things like whale oil.) *However, even a wealthy man like*

Rockefeller can be threatened with a potential crisis.

What was this threat, you wonder? Simple: electricity. The advent of people like Edison and Tesla lead to the emergence of a whole new industry: electricity. Imagine what could have happened if Americans had suddenly decided to switch from kerosene to electricity (perhaps powered by hydro-electricity from dams)? This new industry threatened to inflict a dramatic blow to Rockefeller's profits.

However, did Rockefeller have an ace up his sleeve – his R&D spending? (Note: R&D is nothing more than institutionalized imagination and creativity.) His scientists had apparently come up with a somewhat unstable and combustible new oil product. Unfortunately, its properties did not suggest it could be marketed as a product. It appeared useless. Did this mean his spending on R&D had been wasted?

Not really. As "luck" would have it another disruptive technology hit the scene at around this time, in the guise of Henry Ford and his model T–ushering in a whole new industry: cars for the masses. Now guess what these cars needed? The new oil (gasoline) that Rockefeller's R&D department had discovered! Preparation + opportunity = luck. Rockefeller went on to become even wealthier than before!

Contrast this with the stories of those horse carriage makers who simply assumed the world would never change and never invested in the future. Imagine their dwindling profits when the car industry was invented.

In fact, the world is constantly changing, and curiosity and imagination, are no longer luxuries but rather a necessity. As the saying goes "Innovate or perish."

Boldly thinking "outside the box" can be extraordinarily profitable. One only needs to look at lists of America's richest people – past and present- and how they made their money. One of America's richest was Cornelius Vanderbilt who made his fortune in railroads. Some might say: "Oh he was simply the right person at the right time."

Was he? He easily could have been the wrong person at the wrong time. You see, before he was in railroads, he owned a huge shipping empire. However, when he saw the potential of railroads in opening up America and the enormous ensuing profits, he did not hesitate – he bought. He invested heavily into railroads, funding himself by divesting himself of shipping assets. In the process he made a fortune, and saved himself more than a few headaches. Think outside the box before others do. Preparation + opportunity = luck.

Andrew Carnegie was another giant of American industry. He made his money in steel. Initially, he had become interested in steel because of his involvement in building bridges. He was trying to push the boundaries of bridge construction by building one of the world's longest bridges. To accomplish this task he chose to use steel – whose new properties allowed for the imagination of entirely new bridges. In the process, he learned a great deal about the manufacture, funding, and use of steel.

So, you are thinking, what's the big deal, he made his fortune building bridges, right? Life is not always that simple. You see as "luck" would have it, an entirely new industry, building tall buildings to handle the rapidly increasing urban US population – unexpectedly exploded on the scene. Now guess what they needed to build those tall structures? Yup, Andrew Carnegie's steel. Preparation + opportunity = luck.

Will you work hard to be ready for your opportunities? Will you see the world as your opportunity pipeline? Think outside the box. Increase the surface area for "luck receptors" in your life for "luck" to attach to (at least, a few more than that of your counterparts in life).

> "I've found that luck is quite predictable. If you want more luck, take more chances. Be more active. Show up more often." Brian Tracy

REWARDS OF INNOVATION

Reaping the rewards of Imagination – thinking outside the box

CASE (POLITICS)

Bold, imaginative moves are the hallmarks of major threads in history. We still benefit from the imaginative minds of the Athenians of ancient Greece and from their bold, probing experiments in democracy. Athens in ancient Greece was a cauldron of ideas, and more importantly its citizens were willing to entertain "wild," speculative political experiments.

In one such very early recorded event around 508 BCE, the citizens of Athens tasked their wisest citizen Cleisthenes, to come up with a new form of government. Cleisthenes established a novel system. His primary idea was the creation of "the Council of 500."

Five hundred Athenians would be randomly selected to govern temporarily through this legislative body. The citizens of Athens would enter their names into clay pots from which the council of 500 would be drawn. This method would allow most Athenian citizens to "govern" Athens at least once in their lifetimes by being a member of this council. It is one of the first recorded examples of "rule by the people" or a form of direct democracy.

Interestingly, Cleisthenes also devised an "anti-election." During this particular election, if more than 6,000 wrote down a particular name -that was the top vote getter–that individual could be banished from Athens for ten years. Finally, he also enshrined a form of free speech by allowing any citizen to stand up and speak in front of the general assembly.

It is from this rich nutrient mix in Athens that contemporary democratic ideas have evolved. And while democracies are not perfect, they may curb some of the excesses of some other types of government.

The power of imagination.

CASE – FICTION

Here is an interesting story in ancient Chinese literature. Once an senior army strategist/officer was tasked with the "impossible" task of acquiring and stocking the munitions for an upcoming battle.

A normal person would have looked at the munitions needs versus what was available and simply given up. However the enterprising officer replied that he would have the task done.

This in itself was to say the least, very surprising. However, his next answer was shocking. Not only would he have it done, but he would have it done within a day! Impossible squared, I guess one might say.

So what did the officer do?

Here is what he did:

The officer ordered huge bales of hay to be rolled onto some large wooden boats. Spotting the enemy on nearby river banks, he ordered a surprise attack with his large wooden boats and a contingent of his soldiers onboard. Familiar with weather patterns and local conditions, he waited until an anticipated fog rolled in, before he ordered the boats to move out. The fog would add to the confusion of the surprise attack, he calculated.

Caught off guard, the enemy archers reacted instinctively and released rally after rally of their deadly arrows from the river banks onto the menacing dimly visible oncoming boats.

The officer calmly watched the ensuing battle. Periodically his soldiers had been instructed to beat their war drums, which further agitated the enemy, causing they to respond even more furiously and haphazardly. After watching the spectacle for a time, the officer then abruptly signaled his boats to return to his base.

The next day found the officer directing his troops to extract the hundreds of arrows that had lodged themselves in the bales of hay.

He was asked, "When will the munitions be available?" "Soon," he replied smiling, as he leaned in and extracted yet another arrow.[1]

A great example of thinking outside the box.

CASE (HISTORY)

For our next case of innovative thinking, let's turn to Julius Caesar, the famous Roman conqueror. During Julius Caesar's bloody invasion of Gaul (e.g., France and some neighboring areas), the conqueror laid siege to Alesia in 52 BCE with around 60,000 of his Roman soldiers. Inside Alesia, opposing Caesar, were an estimated 80,000 Gallic warriors lead by Vercingetorix of the Arverni. In consideration of the fact that Alesia was a fort on a hill surrounded by rivers, the Romans wisely decided on a siege instead of a head-on assault.

So Caesar laid siege, building fortifications to trap the Gauls. Then he waited hoping to starve them into submission. While waiting, he received news that a relief force of over 120,000 had been raised to help break the siege.

Many commanders at this point would have broken the siege and left. Not Caesar. Instead he demonstrated his considerable military genius by engaging in an extraordinarily creative and brilliant military maneuver. He ordered the additional construction of outer(!) walls and fortifications. In essence, he created a double set of walls— the inner walls to lay siege, and the outer walls and fortifications to defend his troops

---

1 Loosely describes a story from the famous 14th century Chinese classic "Romance of the Three Kingdoms." That fictionalized story maybe inspired from events in the Battle of Ruxu in 213 CE. (see Weilüe). While fiction, it still is a story that encourages creativity and innovation.

against the approaching relief column.

Then, the relief column arrived. Incredibly, even though he was at times outnumbered four to one, this unusual, dual structure of fortifications allowed him to survive and eventually triumph. Alesia is considered one Julius Caesar's greatest military achievements, and is a classic example of thinking outside the box.

CASE – HISTORY

Conquest of Constantinople

Constantinople, the head of the Byzantine Empire, was heavily fortified–protected by a ring of moats and a powerful system of double walls. Its gulf harbor had a narrow entry point and a heavy chain to control access. The chain was lowered to allow the ships into the gulf, and *when raised, it effectively prevented any unauthorized entry.* The city was sealed tight.

Constantinople had been unconquered for many centuries, and its formidable defenses seemed to suggest it would remain unconquered. As such, when a young, 21-year-old Ottomon sultan named Mehmet II announced an invasion plan, it was greeted with a healthy dose of skepticism. However, conquer he did and the way he did it shows an amazing ability to think outside the box.

The chain barrier had been impregnable, completely shielding the harbor from the sultan's navy. So what did the sultan do? He simply ignored it. Instead, his large naval sailing ships completely bypassed the water entry into the harbor and sailed towards the shore.

He then executed his plan. One by one, the big, mighty

31

ships of the fleet were pulled out of the water by teams of oxen and men, straining mightily and pulling long, large ropes bringing the ungainly ships onto long rows of constructed planks. Next, the men and animals slogged away, pulling the ships along the ground, using rows of wooden beams to slide the bottom of the ships across.

Making matters worse, the ground was not flat. The bands of toiling men and oxen actually needed to drag the fleet of lumbering, heavy ships up a hill to the other side: the protected gulf harbor. When they had finished they succeeded in pulling off one of the most unexpected, creative military maneuvers in history. The arrival of the Ottoman fleet in the protective Constantinople harbor gulf completely caught the inhabitants of the fortified town by surprise.

This team was clearly determined to win. In the days that followed, the sultan's men, aided by advanced cannon technology, breached the walls and entered the city victoriously and made history in the process. A classic case of thinking outside the box.

Moral of the story: When you sail into a roadblock in life, figure out how to "fly" your sailing ship over the obstacle.

CASE – BUSINESS

One of the mistakes people sometimes make is becoming too creative before learning one's craft or the "rules of the game." As the saying goes, learn the rules of the game before you try to break them.

"You have to learn the rules of the game. And then you

have to play better than anyone else." Albert Einstein

What would you do if you woke up one morning to find that a competitor was trying to put you out of business by slashing prices on products you were selling?

What if it was completely unexpected, and coming from abroad?

Let's make it even more dramatic: Let's make the competitor's selling price below your cost! Thus your bankruptcy is a real possibility.

Many people would panic. Perhaps they would frantically call upon their local politicians to immediately pass some laws to protect local businesses. However, let's try a completely different approach: why don't we try to think outside the box? Try to brainstorm some creative solutions. What could one do if placed in this unfortunate situation?

Herbert Henry Dow, born in 1866, was the founder of Dow Chemical. Early in his career, he had invented a new extraction technique for bromine and had set up a new company. His new, streamlined and cost-effective techniques allowed him to sell bromine at 36 cents per pound. Soon, he was eyeing foreign markets. Bromine, at that time, was controlled by a German cartel, Bromkonvention. Unsurprisingly, when he began to expand into England and Japan, he caught the ire of the cartel. The cartel decided they would put this upstart out of business, and they began dumping bromine on the U.S. market at 15 cents a pound. They expected the quick demise of Dow's venture.

Did Dow panic? Did he go out of business? No, and no. In a brilliant stroke of genius, Dow began to buy

33

(not sell!) bromine. Then, in a cleverly disguised set of maneuvers, he sold the massive quantities of bromine he bought into the German market at 27 cents a pound pocketing the large spread (27 minus 15) as pure profit - a profit financed entirely by his competition. The cartel had no idea what had hit them. By the time the bromine cartel figured out what was going on, it was too late. Dow had triumphed.

Dow went on to become very successful. Nowadays, Dow's maneuver is sometimes cited as a classic way on how to combat "predatory pricing".

In any case, it was a dramatic example of thinking outside the box.

Note:

I like to think of Dow's move as "business judo," i.e., using someone else's energy against themselves.

BEING IMAGINATIVE

Is imagination hard work?

Have you ever felt lazy? C'mon, you can admit it. We all have. It's a part of human nature.

Wouldn't it be great if you could put that feeling to some good use? How, you wonder, can laziness be put to good use? Intrigued? Read on.

> "I choose a lazy person to do a hard job. Because a lazy person will find an easy way to do it." Bill Gates[2]

Yup – surprise, surprise; laziness can be incredibly inventive. (This is something most kids discover pretty

---

[2]   Usually attributed to Gates. Idea may have origins in efficiency expert Frank B. Gilbreth Sr. but probably goes back thousands of years :)

early in life).

Caveat: In order for this technique to be more useful, it helps if one is generally honest, smart and motivated.

THE EASY WAY TO BE ORIGINAL — BE YOURSELF

"Formal education will make you a living; self-education will make you a fortune." Jim Rohn

"If a man does not keep pace with his companions, perhaps it is because he hears a different drummer. Let him step to the music which he hears, however measured or far away." Henry David Thoreau

"Do not go where the path may lead, go instead where there is no path and leave a trail." Ralph Waldo Emerson

"The more you like yourself, the less you are like anyone else, which makes you unique." Walt Disney

"Originality is unexplored territory. You get there by carrying a canoe — you can't take a taxi." Alan Alda

If you only go where everyone has already been, you will live in an over-crowded, hyper competitive, severely depleted place. Why go where all the gold has already been mined? Instead, build your own worlds where the sky is the limit, and there are many kinds of worlds. Even taking an old world and adding a tiny, little, original twist creates an entirely new world.

"To be yourself in a world that is constantly trying to make you something else is the greatest accomplishment." Ralph Waldo Emerson

There is only one person like you who has existed or

will exist. Be unique. Find yourself. Be yourself. Do not deprive the world of your unique gifts, experiences, and world view. Just imagine how dull (and hyper competitive) the world would be if everyone was a clone of one person. The world is vibrant and dynamic because of its different sounds, smells, hues and vibrations. Build a world of color, not a black and white world, and add your unique touch to the world. Be yourself.

INNOVATION GUIDE: EXPLORE CREATIVITY

"This world is but a canvas to our imagination." Henry David Thoreau

Here are some ideas/practice exercises on becoming more creative, imaginative.

1. Be relaxed. Have fun. Play. Don't overly analyze (while being creative). It's much easier to be creative under these conditions. Alternatively, if stressed out, sleep on it. The next day, your brain may find it easier to make new connections.

2. Translate from one world to another.

» (Temporal) Retell a story set in the Roman Empire to modern day Wall Street or vice versa.

» (Species/Movie) Watch a nature program. Translate the animals to people from a movie and vice versa.

» (Personal) Translate from World War II (WWII) to your industry. Have fun trying to find out which WWII personality maps to which industrial figure or family member. Be nice!

Essentially we are talking about using combinatorics for inspiration in the last few lines above. Mix up locales, times, real world, animals, people, fictional characters, and *whatever other variables (or combination of dimensions) you can think of* to fuel your imagination. [3]

The resulting mishmash can be funny, amazing, or a dud. Enjoy!

3. Flip. Turn things upside down and inside out. Use your imagination. For example, imagine if one day all the rich people woke up poor and all the poor people were rich. What kind of a day would it be if everyone knew it would only last for a day? What if you considered poor nations instead of poor people or ten years instead of a day? Have fun. Be outlandish in your thoughts.

4. Have super creative, supportive friends. Creativity is like yawning: it's contagious. Feed off each other's fun thoughts.

5. Be a supportive friend. Be on the receiving end -help others be creative. Let them bounce their crazy ideas off you. Interestingly if you help others be creative over a long enough time period, you will begin to acquire a more intuitive sense of what works (and what is less likely to work) in terms of creativity.

6. Intellectually entertain "stupid" ideas. After laughing through some obviously ridiculous concepts, you may find yourself beginning to home in on some good

---

3   For more spice: add constraints, losses and/or remove assumptions.

ideas.

> I have not failed. I've just found 10,000 ways that won't work. Thomas A. Edison

7. *Consider the saying: One man's junk, is another man's treasure.* Look for things you want, and see who might be looking to get rid of it and might give it to you for free. Can be a very interesting exercise (or a new way of creative thinking).

8. *Imagine "impossible," very unique, or funny things.* Consider centaurs from mythology. Centaurs were half human, half horse. What qualities or traits come to mind when you think of a horse or a human? Which person do you know that combines these traits? What combination of traits tickles you or ignites your curiosity? For example, a lion that roars is not nearly as interesting a character for a book as a "cowardly lion[4]." Try to image the most fascinating characters you can for a children's book. Play with their names too.

9. *Exaggerate.* Humor and imagination are linked. Take an ordinary situation and wildly exaggerate some aspect of it to make your friends laugh.

10. *Explore your different emotions.* Emotions can be powerful weapons to unleash creative bursts.

11. *Dramatically increase the diversity you are exposed to in life.* Seek more diversity in friends. Engage in wider conversations. Expose yourself to new cultures. Create new experiences in your life. Vary your routine. Add spontaneity to your life. These things will help you become more naturally creative.

4   Wizard of Oz?

12. Try improvisational comedy.

13. Read books; see movies in an imaginative genre like science fiction. See how other people are creative. Maybe it will light a spark under you.

14. Collect your creative thoughts. Ideas can come at any time. Have an easy way to jot down ideas whenever they strike.

15. Practice. The more you work on something the better you will become at it.

Bonus tip: One fun thing I have done personally in the past is to stop a movie (or tv show) periodically, and then predict what will happen next. It can be: hilarious, done alone, with family/friends. In the long run, I have found it to be a great creativity booster.

EXERCISE #1

Select one of the ways to be creative from the innovation guide above. Try it out. Repeat, as necessary.

SUMMARY

- Preparation + opportunity = luck
- Practice thinking outside the box
- Imagination can be a super-ingredient for success.
- Be unique; be yourself
- Use the innovation guide periodically

Chapter 3
Understanding Failure: Risk, Criticism, & Persistence

WHY A CHAPTER ABOUT FAILURE?

Well, my answer is really quite simple. If you can conquer failure, what can possibly conquer you?

Everyone will fail at least once (probably more) in their lives. It is unavoidable. Why not try to understand failure, risk, criticism, and persistence, and at least learn a little from the process?

LOSS AVERSION

Studying failure can expose interesting cognitive pathways in our minds. Let us examine something called prospect theory. "Prospect theory" arises from behavioral economics, which is a field that lies at the intersection of psychology and economics. It suggests that many people may choose to weigh losses more heavily than gains. It suggests that due to something called "loss aversion," you may be happier if someone gave you $25,000, rather than giving you $50,000 and then asking for $25,000 back. You would actually be happier in the first case, even though you ended up with the same amount of money in both cases.

Many people have an aversion to loss. Sometimes, it is tucked away deep in the human mind.

THE PROBLEM: EVEN "SAFE" SCHEMES CAN HAVE COSTS

Sure, one could put one's money under one's mattress and protect it from a dangerous world, and one could lock oneself inside one's house to escape all the potential dangers of the world. After all, even crossing a street is dangerous. However, here's the rub: one cannot do these things in a vacuum. An honest analysis requires one to analyze those measures more deeply.

Specifically, what if one had made a different decision? How would one have fared differently in life? How differently? For example, how would one have fared differently by taking a small amount of risk with one's money by investing it into some productive asset? Alternatively, how would things be different by going out into the world to seek some good.

Economics actually has a name for this analysis: determining opportunity costs. In other words, in order to properly evaluate these "safe" schemes, one needs to calculate the cost of lost opportunities. In other words, in making a decision, how much might it COST you to ignore an alternative OPPORTUNITY? Hence , we have the term OPPORTUNITY COST.

Now ask yourself what are the real costs of taking "no risk." For example in the contrived example above, one might argue that *fear of failure may itself be a potential source of failure.* For example, in an environment of high inflation, the money-under-the-mattress approach may leave one with barely enough to survive during retirement. Yet, an alternative, more active investment of that money might leave one better able to cope with retirement.

41

WHAT IS FAILURE?

Failure is often misunderstood

DISAPPOINTMENTS CAN BE A MIRAGE

Did you know that the original day for D-Day, the landings in Normandy for the Allied invasion of Europe was June 5th, 1944? Yet it was delayed by 24 hours to June 6th on account of weather. Was it disappointing, frustrating, and aggravating to the people involved? Perhaps.

Due to the need for low tide, and a full moon, the potential dates for a landing were limited. Months of preparation had already been expended. Tension was already razor sharp. Then the delay came, i.e., the stressful news of the bad weather.

Was it disheartening? Was it unfortunate for the Allies? Maybe not. Let's examine what actually happened.

In a brilliant (and lucky) piece of weather forecasting, the British meteorologists predicted that there would be a short lull in the poor weather on June 6th, which would allow for the Normandy landings. However, because the weather was so bad, the *German forecasters predicted the opposite:* that the Allies would be unlikely to take any action during that time period. The Germans were so relaxed that Field Marshall Rommel even left France to return home to Germany.

The potential disappointment, i.e., the bad weather, was not really a disappointment! Instead, it was the source of great fortune for the Allies. It was one of the factors that allowed them to launch a completely unexpected surprise invasion.[1]

Good Luck or Bad Luck–Who Knows?

There is an ancient Chinese fable that goes something like this:

There once was a poor, old farmer who lived on a small plot of land. Every day, he would wake up early and together with his trusty horse would plow his fields.

One day, he woke up and found his horse gone. His neighbor was concerned about the farmer's loss, and tried to console him, but the farmer simply replied,

"Good luck or bad luck–who knows?"

When the sun rose on the farmer's land the next day it revealed that his horse had returned with a companion. The farmer now had two horses. The neighbor remarked on this remarkable turn of fortune. The farmer simply replied,

"Good luck or bad luck–who knows?"

The next day, excited by the prospect of a new horse, the farmer's only son decided to try to tame and ride the new horse. His attempt quickly ended when he was thrown off the horse and broke his leg. Again, the farmer's neighbor lamented on the farmer's change of fortune, and again the farmer's reply was the same,

"Good luck or bad luck -who knows?"

Now as fate would have it, the next day an army rolled

---

1   You can read an interesting account of D-Day and the weather forecasts on http://www.history.com/news/the-weather-forecast-that-saved-d-day

into the village. They forcibly seized every able-bodied boy in the village to serve in their ranks. Being lame, the farmer's boy was spared.

Moral of the story: It is sometimes difficult to know if something is good or bad for you.

ARE SUCCESS AND FAILURE LINKED TOGETHER IN SOME WAY?

"All the adversity I've had in my life, all my troubles and obstacles, have strengthened me... You may not realize it when it happens, but a kick in the teeth may be the best thing in the world for you." Walt Disney

"Failure is not the opposite of success, it's part of success." Arianna Huffington

"Failure is where success likes to hide in plain sight." Scott Adams

"Behind a great success, there was a great failure." Michael Hermanto

Most of us understand this concept intuitively. Watch any movie; read any fiction story: if the hero or heroine immediately gets what he or she is seeking (without any setbacks) what would the audience say? Perhaps it would be: "How unrealistic" or "Not in my life!"

Life has trained us to this simple concept, expressed by Henry David Thoreau, "Truths and roses have thorns about them."

IN ORDER TO UNDERSTAND FAILURE, ONE NEEDS TO ADOPT A PROPER MINDSET

"If," a famous poem by Kipling, has an interesting take

on "success" and "failure". Here it is.

If

By Rudyard Kipling

If you can keep your head when all about you

Are losing theirs and blaming it on you,

If you can trust yourself when all men doubt you,

But make allowance for their doubting too;

If you can wait and not be tired by waiting,

Or being lied about, don't deal in lies,

Or being hated, don't give way to hating,

And yet don't look too good, nor talk too wise:

If you can dream—and not make dreams your master;

If you can think—and not make thoughts your aim;

If you can meet with Triumph and Disaster

And treat those two impostors just the same;

If you can bear to hear the truth you've spoken

Twisted by knaves to make a trap for fools,

Or watch the things you gave your life to, broken,

And stoop and build 'em up with worn-out tools:

If you can make one heap of all your winnings

And risk it on one turn of pitch-and-toss,

And lose, and start again at your beginnings

And never breathe a word about your loss;

If you can force your heart and nerve and sinew

To serve your turn long after they are gone,

And so hold on when there is nothing in you

Except the Will which says to them: "Hold on!"

If you can talk with crowds and keep your virtue,

Or walk with Kings—nor lose the common touch,

If neither foes nor loving friends can hurt you,

If all men count with you, but none too much;

If you can fill the unforgiving minute

With sixty seconds' worth of distance run,

Yours is the Earth and everything that's in it,

And—which is more—you'll be a Man, my son.

What did you think of the poem? Even though it was written a long time ago, it remains a fascinating poem.

STEPPING STONES

"The innovator's motto is this; I succeed or I learn but I never fail." Paul Sloane

"Every adversity, every failure, every heartache carries with it the seed on an equal or greater benefit." Napoleon Hill

CASE – POLITICS

Even when you fail, do you really fail?

Consider the case of U.S. president Woodrow Wilson and the League of Nations. The League of Nations was the first global organization founded and entrusted with the primary task of maintaining world peace. Unfortunately, it suffered from numerous shortcomings.

For example, although having been proposed by an American president (Woodrow Wilson), the U.S.A. was not a member. This and similar flaws became painfully obvious when the League of Nations had little or no effect in preventing World War II (WWII).

Some might view the League of Nations as a failure. However, I would advance that it was not a complete failure, in the sense that it laid the vital seeds for future success: its successor, the new and improved "United Nations."

The experience of WWII made clear the value of a global body. Nations did learn from the failures of the League of Nations, and its successor, the United Nations, rectified many of the League's shortcomings.

In a sense the League was an intermediate step– a vital link between propelling a dream forward to what was possible, While the United Nations (U.N.) is not perfect, it is a step forward, and hopefully the U.N. itself will continue to improve.

CASE – AGING

Many older people find that learning how to handle life's challenges contributed to their long-term happiness. The skills acquired and the mental and emotional growth from tackling problems made them stronger, happier, and more resilient.

"Failure is a learning experience." Thomas Edison.

GROWTH

> Tom Watson, Sr., (of IBM fame) said, "If you want to succeed, double your failure rate."

> "Unless you try to do something beyond what you have already mastered, you will never grow." Ralph Waldo Emerson

If you want to grow, it is difficult to do so without ever experiencing failure. It is a concept that even a child can readily grasp. Consider when you first learnt to ride a bike. Sure, you were scared and uncertain at first. Perhaps, you fell a couple of times, but eventually you did it. You managed to successfully ride your bike, and what a wonderful feeling it was!

> "Failure always brings something valuable with it. I don't let it leave until I extract that value. " Scott Adams

CASE – BUSINESS PERSON

How a specific kind of failure (mindset) made Sara a success:

Sara Blakely

» wanted to be a lawyer, but failed the LSAT twice

» then tried out for Goofy at Disney World, but failed because of her height

» For seven years, she went door-to-door selling fax machines

» never took a business class prior to her success

» had not worked previously in retail or fashion

» started a business with $5,000 in savings

» In 2012, Blakely was named the world's youngest, self-made, female billionaire

» By 2013, retail sales were over $500 million

Are you wondering what she credits for her incredible financial success? It is her attitude towards failure. Specifically she credits her father for teaching her that failure is an important ingredient in eventual success.

Blakely vividly remembers her father asking her and her brother on the dinner table "What did you fail at this week?" *If she did not say anything he would be disappointed.*

Eventually, those conversations redefined failure for her to simply mean not trying, as opposed to not succeeding. It reset her mindset.

It taught her, for example, not to give up when the manufacturers she approached about her "crazy idea" did not know how to respond to her. It also helped her land her first sales since she had the drive to fly over to the buyer to personally present her idea.

It did not take long for Sara to achieve financial success. In 2012, Blankely was named the world's youngest, self-made, female billionaire.

PERSISTENCE

"Success is stumbling from failure to failure with no loss of enthusiasm." Winston Churchill

"When I was young, I observed that nine out of ten things I did were failures. So I did ten times more work." George Bernard Shaw

"If you want success, figure out the price, then pay it." Scott Adams

"We did it in Disneyland, in the knowledge that most of the people I talked to thought it would be a financial disaster–closed and forgotten within the first year." Walt Disney

WALT DISNEY

Here are some interesting things about Walt Disney. Did you know that:

» Disney dropped out of high school at the age of sixteen

» Nobody would initially hire him as an artist

» At least two companies that he started failed

» He lost most of his staff and his main cartoon character in a corporate dispute, which compelled him to create a new character, Mickey Mouse.

» His first full length feature, "Snow White," was called "Disney's Folly" by his competitors. Even his wife and brother tried to talk him out of the film, and he ran out of money before it was finished. Yet, it went on to become the best movie of 1938 and helped firmly establish him.

The above chronology clearly shows Disney's persistence, for which he was rewarded. By the 1960s, Disney was regarded as one of the world's leading producers of family entertainment with more Oscar awards (22) and nominations (59) than any other individual in history.

FAILURE–IT'S A TEMPORARY THING.

"A hero is no braver than an ordinary man, but he is brave five minutes longer." Ralph Waldo Emerson

"Our greatest glory is not in never failing, but in rising up every time we fail." Ralph Waldo Emerson

FAILURE IS NOT PERMANENT

WASHINGTON AT TRENTON

By the fall of 1776, General George Washington was reeling from a string of defeats and retreats across New York and New Jersey at the hands of the pursing victorious British forces.

By December 1776, across the Delaware River in Pennsylvania, the situation had turned dire. Washington had lost 90% of his army. What was left was a ragged, poorly supplied motley crew of hungry, freezing, and demoralized men. Most critically, most of the few remaining soldiers were to have their enlistments expire on January 1st. Come 1777, it was uncertain if Washington would even have an army.

The British themselves expected to mop up the remaining Americans in the upcoming spring. The future of the American experiment was dark and uncertain.

Against this backdrop Washington took a bold, unorthodox winter move and attacked 1,500 Hessian forces under Colonel Rall that were serving the British and that were stationed in Trenton, NJ. Even with a reduced troop complement, this surprise attack routed the Hessians and garnered Washington a badly

51

needed victory.

Trenton served as a dramatic psychological boost, and brought the American experiment back from the brink of collapse. Most importantly, it resumed the critical flow of new recruits to the cause. Despite the small size of the victory, it was a decisive, pivotal turning point in the American revolutionary war of independence.[2]

"Success is not final, failure is not fatal: it is the courage to continue that counts." Winston Churchill

LEVERING FAILURE/CRITICISM

"A successful man is one who can lay a firm foundation with the bricks others have thrown at him." David Brinkley

Don't accept failure; leverage it! Use failure to actually build success. Don't despair. Listen to factual criticism, especially if it is from a competitor. Oops ... looks like they just told you precisely how to beat them!

BE OPEN TO GOOD THINGS BEING HIDDEN ALL AROUND YOU

But beware, and heed this warning.

Warning: opportunities come with expiration dates

FAILURE WITH CLASS

If you have been dealt bad cards play the cards you have the best way you can. You might find that people will respect you for it. At any rate, defeat is a state of

---

2   Learn more about the importance of this and other decisive events from the excellent work of people like Gregory S. Aldrete, if interested.

mind. Try to endure it with dignity. Defeat or no defeat, for both will come one's way, the victor should see a worthy opponent.

Athletes are well aware of this. It is considered a sign of good/bad sportsmanship to show good/poor behavior upon a loss. No one likes a sore loser.

REWARDS

It's okay for you to espouse on these issues, but how about someone great? How about some of the smartest people in the world?

Actually, one can go even beyond merely seeing what people say, but actually noting where they have put their money.

Just look at the venture capital industry, the research process for medical discoveries, or R&D in general. Each is littered with an abundance of "failures", yet, billions of dollars and thousands of hours continue to be poured into these endeavors by extremely smart people.

Why do very bright minds spend billions of dollars in fields littered with failure? Simple, they expect even greater successes to offset those "failures." In fact, the last few years have seen massively disruptive technologies change the face of things, and medical advances been driven forward.

> "Science, my lad, is made up of mistakes, but they are mistakes which it is useful to make, because they lead little by little to the truth." Jules Verne, Journey to the Center of the Earth

"The impediment to action advances action. What stands in the way becomes the way. " Marcus Aurelius

Smart people understand the extraordinary rewards of taking calculated risks.

MANAGEMENT OF RISK

Here are some possible ideas about the management of risk[3].

Try to come up with your own list. The list you eventually come up with for yourself may well be different than this one.

Types of failure (one time or repeatable)

One useful cue might be whether the errors are irreversible. Do you live in an environment of "second chances," or a more unforgiving one? If you find your situation resonates with the saying, "No second chances to make a first impression," it might be the latter.

While one can sometimes maneuver oneself into a more forgiving environment, this may not always be possible. Structurally, time and death are two examples. If one has made a string of poor decisions over a long period, barring the invention of a time machine, it may be very difficult to maneuver into a better situation. Alternately, upon death, one's actions are fixed, regrets and all.

Generally speaking, repeatable scenarios allow for a little more "risk" than "one-time" unforgiving scenar-

---

3   The comfort level of risk is a very personal thing, these are simply ideas upon which to ruminate. They may or may not apply to you. This list is by no means comprehensive or exhaustive.

ios.

COST OF THE ERROR

Taking a chance and being rejected by a member of the opposite gender does not typically involve the same level of consequences as doing medical experiments on oneself, the latter of which is generally a very bad idea. Not paying attention while driving (a bad idea): another example of a possible error with very high potential costs. Higher costs, of course, discourage risk.

Incurring high costs relative to potential rewards or expecting small rewards relative to high costs is usually not worth it. What's even worse is, if the rewards are short-lived and the costs are long-term e.g. a 30 second thrill balanced against a life long injury.

The pendulum shifts for many people more towards risk when the impact or reward can be dramatic and the costs manageable, low, and short-term.

RECOVERY AND ALTERNATIVES

Being surrounded by wealth or poverty, living with a safety net versus without one, being younger versus being older are considerations influencing how resilient you can be. This in turn can influence the level of risk with which you might be comfortable.

SOME STRATEGIES

» If you might hit a dry hole, dig many small holes to try to mitigate your risk.

» Develop "resilience muscles," e.g. a support network, a backup skillset, the right mental attitude, doing sports, being a great spouse, having a great spouse, exercising, etc.

» Diversify. Diversify risk. For example, many professionals in the finance industry face risk. One tactic used is to diversify, to better control the risk.

» Strategically spread out smaller potential failures to protect against bigger potential failures. Many startups place a number of smaller bets to "sniff out the market" before committing themselves to large bets.

When does it pay to take a bigger risk?

One scenario might be that when one is way behind (e.g., the competition has a commanding lead), the risk of action is bracketed, and there will be a definite resolution within a specific time frame.

In an earlier period in my life, I used to sail in New York City. At that time, I had been interested in racing sailboats, and had learnt a few different strategies. One strategy dealt with what to do if your sail boat was far behind all the other boats.

Essentially at that point, you had no hope of winning. Since the only point of the race was to win, basically one had two choices: go through the motions and complete the race in the spirit of good sportsmanship, or take a dramatic risk. At that point, it was a no-brainer . Anything you did could not make your situation worse, i.e. you were already going to lose. There was no downside, but there was a huge upside if the risk paid off and you won.

At this point, a short digression into the mechanics of

sailing might be useful. Sailing, unlike motor boating, is heavily dependent on the wind. Maneuverability and speed are directly related to local wind direction and strength. As such, racing strategy does depend on predictions about wind conditions during the course of a race. In our scenario, we could hope for a dramatically different series of wind events than what the other boats were expecting, i.e. the prevailing wisdom.

In order to capitalize, we could attempt, for example, to place our boat far out to the right of all the other boats. If we were very lucky and the wind conditions changed relatively in our favor, our boat would gain on all the others.

How does this idea translate into other aspects of life? One example might be amazon. When the ecommerce startup amazon.com first emerged on the scene, it was a tiny spec compared to industry behemoths like brick and mortar book retail Barnes and Noble and others.

Its strategy for market domination was diametrically different than traditional retailers. The winds (of radical technological shifts) propelled amazon growth far more rapidly than its competitors. It had greatly benefited from shifts in the landscape by adopting an entirely different business (internet-based) strategy than its competitors.

FAILURE AND EXPERIMENTS

"All life is an experiment. The more experiments you make the better." Ralph Waldo Emerson

Why not apply the "scientific method" continuously, cheaply, and often in everyday life? What is the scientific method? It simply says if you are not sure of something, why not come up with a hypothesis (or intelligent guess) for what you think might be the answer. Then create an experiment to test that guess to see if you were right.

Startups often begin as hunches in a founder's mind. However, until the product meets the market, the outcome of the experiment is uncertain. "Lean startups" follow the mantra "build, measure, and learn." In the "lean philosophy"[4] one tries to accelerate the experiment outcome in order to manage the risk of failure.

Instead of fully building out a product, they try to create a MVP (minimum viable product). In other words, the minimum required to establish whether there is a product-market fit. The product may lack "bells and whistles" but it may have just enough skeleton features to let you know (most crucially) if there is actually a sufficient market demand for your core product.

Thus, by building a MVP, and measuring the market demand, one can learn how to proceed. By reviewing market feedback, one may find that the "round widget with a blue bow" has no future, but that the customers loved the blue bow. Since you spent so little money in producing the MVP, you still have enough resources to switch over to producing blue bows only. Switching or re-tuning your products in midstream is called "pivoting." Startups can go through a few pivots during "build, measure, and learn" cycles before finding the right product and market, before they begin to scale.

This approach is better than simply perfecting your

4   If interested in lean startups, check out Steve Blank's Lean Startup course at udacity.

product, building ten factories, and finding out that only three people want to buy your "perfect" original product. That would probably count as a "failure."

The "build, measure, and learn" mantra goes beyond finding a product-market fit. In the age of the internet, with copious amounts of data and ubiquitous software, it is very easy and cheap to craft experiments to answer basic marketing questions. For example, marketers experiment with background colors, fonts, images, titles, and copy on product detail pages to determine how they influence buying behavior. One can obtain very precise answers (within certain statistical parameters) about how much more profitable title1 is versus title2 or image1 versus image2 when associated with a product. Futhermore, this process can often be cheap, quick, and easy.

At its heart, this process attempts to reduce risk dramatically (i.e. minimize the risk of a huge failure) by continuously running tiny, cheap data experiments and engaging in numerous course corrections to move towards the right direction.

SUMMARY

- Trying too hard to avoid failure can sometimes lead to failure
- Failure can be a mirage
- Treat failure as a stepping stone
- Find success behind failure
- Create a proper mind-set
- Failure is temporary; get back up

- Persistence is important
- There can be great rewards
- Learn to mange risk
- Learning to handle failure well can became a super-ingredient for success

Chapter 4
How to beat the smartest person in the room?

Have you ever wondered how you could beat the smartest person in the room?

It's simple. Use a team. Even the smartest person cannot be at two places at once, or excel at finance, law, operations, marketing, technology, etc. simultaneously. It's a surprisingly simple concept, but it's very effective.

This might be one reason one finds some "C" (e.g., "average") students excelling later in life. In many cases, they have assembled teams of "A" (e.g., high performing) students reporting to them, being fully aware of their own limitations. On the other hand, one can find "A" students who are so used to success that they try to go it alone and then struggle when faced with a well-assembled team.

It pays to understand the importance of teams early in life. This is so much so, that this chapter will focus on the value of the working with others. In this regard, we will focus on ideas from a variety of disciplines.

CASE: ARTIFICIAL INTELLIGENCE (MACHINE LEARNING)

There is an interesting result in machine learning – a discipline in computer science that attempts to create "machines" that become "smarter" by "learning" from an ever increasing pool of data. In one type of learning, machines vote amongst themselves, and in truly democratic style the majority decision is the one taken. The amazing result is that even if the individual machines are rather dumb, the overall "cohort of machines" is actually quite smart.

It is a very interesting result. This is because it is very difficult to build a very "smart machine". However, stringing together 101 moderately "smart" "machines" is quite cheap and easy. Here's an illustration: Suppose the machines are "independent" and that each "moderately smart" machine is right on average only 70% of the time. Amazingly, if one strings them together as a group, their collective accuracy can rise to around 99.99%![1] It's quite an fascinating result, wouldn't you say?

Intuitively, one sees this in life when a diverse group of people try to solve a problem. While each individually might not know much about solving the problem, their average sum knowledge of the problem stops them from making a colossal error, and it instead helps them to arrive at a reasonably good solution.

FABLE

There is an ancient Indian fable about an elephant and four blind men. The four blind men approach an

[1]   Assuming a number of things like independence, then the probability that the group will be wrong is a cumulative binomial distribution probability(50 for minority, 101 obs, .7 prob) = .0001. To get the probability of success, subtract this from 1. Ans = .9999. (Actually even with only 51 machines, it goes up to .9986 using this same analysis). Incidentally, this is called ensemble machine learning, and bagging and random forests are two such examples of machine learning techniques.

elephant for the first time. One grabs the elephant's leg, and says that elephants are like giant trees. Another latches on to the elephant's trunk and exclaims that his friend is wrong and that elephants are in fact cousins of snakes. The third is struck by the elephant's ears and cries that they are dealing with giant fans. The fourth berates that other three upon examining the tail. "You are all wrong," he says emphatically. "We are simply dealing with a piece of rope!"

Now, they are all individually terribly wrong. However, in aggregate, they are much closer to the truth. It's the power of teams![2]

STUDY (PSYCHOLOGY)

One of the powerful tangible benefits of diverse teams is to prevent a phenomenon know as group think. This is a condition where we are excessively affected by the biases, shared stories, culture and information of the group of people with whom we identify. This effect is often fairly subtle, and often one is not particularly conscious of being "biased."

Our minds have their own natural rules. Psychology has exposed some of the interesting blind spots in the ways our minds work.

In an interesting 1951 study, researchers analyzed a football game between the Dartmouth Indians and Princeton Tigers. This game was a particularly violent one, with the Princeton quarterback suffering a

---

2   Ok for you science enthusiasts out there, here is something similar: Was not the ideal gas law in chemistry initially seen as different laws e.g. Boyle's law, Charles's law, Avogadro's law, but all essentially really referred to the same equation? Or how about Maxwell's brilliant equations that unified electricity and magnetism?

concussion and broken nose, and a Dartmouth player breaking a leg. The two researchers independently asked a group of Princetonians and Dartmouth students about which side played more roughly. *Even though they had seen exactly the same game*, twice as many students from Princeton than the Dartmouth group indicated that the Dartmouth side had played rougher.

This classic study was one of the first to explore how one's in-built biases might result in the same information being viewed differently. What we recall and emphasize is not "raw reality," but information filtered and viewed through our unique frames.

While a sporting event may seem a trivial example, it does raise the greater question of the difficulty of remaining impartial when faced with the unconscious filtering of information and how one's in-built biases result in the same information being interpreted differently.

It is not unusual, for example, when watching news events with people of different backgrounds, to see events perceived through the prism of personal, pre-set opinions and experiences. Nor does this need to be intentional or malicious. Sometimes, simple hidden cognitive blind spots may help explain selective perception or even the construction of different realities.

Having read the above, consider the following exercise:

Rewrite below:

A professor wrote the following phrase before his

classroom, and asked his students to correctly punctuate it.

"A woman without her man is nothing"

The first group wrote:

"A woman, without her man, is nothing"

The second group wrote:

"A woman: without her, man is nothing"

-Source Unknown

CASE: ECONOMICS

The extraordinary value of other people.

Sam: "All this team talk is just too mushy. It's just easier to do things alone."

Judy: "How could I convince you otherwise? For example, have you ever thought why trade is such a fundamental feature of human societies going back thousands of years?"

Sam: "Well, I suppose some countries had poor agricultural lands and used things like iron ore or salt to procure food, and vice versa."

Judy: "Okay. Let's up the ante. Let's make my case for trade virtually impossible to win. What if your country does EVERYTHING better than my hypothetical country? Would it be profitable for you to ever trade with my country?"

Sam: "That's ridiculous. If we do EVERYTHING better, what use do we have for you? I would never trade with you!"

65

Judy: "If I convince you to trade even under such extreme situations, would you agree that perhaps one should not always go it alone?"

Sam: "Maybe."

Judy: "Fine. Allow me to refer to one of the world's most famous classical economists, David Ricardo. His very influential work notes that even if your country does everything better than others, your country probably does some things comparatively MUCH better than other nations."

Sam: "I guess if my country had so much gold that one could just scratch around pretty much anywhere to uncover it, we would be far ahead of other countries in that regard."

Judy: "Let us suppose we have gold in my country but its two miles below the surface and difficult to excavate. It would cost a lot to produce, but you should buy silver from us."

Sam: "Yeah, your gold would cost 20x more than ours, so I would never buy it. But why would I buy your silver? We produce silver more efficiently than you, and I can produce it 10% cheaper than you. (You did say we did everything better.)"

Judy: "Okay. Consider this idea. Why not simply move your silver miners to mining gold. Then to meet your silver needs, simply trade us your gold for our silver. Sure, you lose 10% on the silver, but you could conceivably gain up to 20x (e.g., 2000%) on your gold. Overall, you are ahead."

Sam: "Hey, you tricked me."

Judy: "It's simply a constraint of time. When you switch your people from silver to gold it reflects the fact that they cannot simultaneously produce gold and silver. So even though you are better at silver than I am, you will use me to meet your silver needs. It can be a win-win situation for the both of us, if we split the resulting gains."[3]

—-

Moral of the story: Working together sure beats "going it alone."

THE TREMENDOUS VALUE OF DIVERSITY ON TEAMS

Most people recognize obvious benefits of diversity on teams. For example, when building a business, it would make no sense just to have marketers on the team. Logically, having a mix of designers, engineers, marketers, and legal and financial people would make much more sense.[4]

THERE IS A STRONG CAVEAT AGAINST DIVERSITY ON TEAMS.

Homogenous teams set up faster and require less training to perform harmoniously. Diverse teams require significant investment in time and resources to begin to perform well. In the absence of such nourishment, diverse teams can end up being very dysfunctional. As such, diverse teams are more likely to end

---

3   Profit distribution and allocation, if appropriate may be a separate question.

4   Here's another example of the value of diversity: the famous Irish potato famine (1845-49 CE). Only one (or two) potato varieties had been planted in most areas. This large decrease in genetic variety greatly increased the crop susceptibility to disease. The crop was wiped out by a blight caused by the HERB-1 strain of Phytophthora infestans, causing widespread famine and misery.

up both at the top and bottom of the pack. Homogenous teams perform at a more consistent mean. However, additional, intelligent effort spent on enhancing diversity may propel a team to the top in the long run.

CASE: PERSONAL

My experience in business school.

When I was studying for my MBA degree, a significant portion of our work was done in teams. It was a two-year program with numerous team assignments every semester.

As people would scramble to join teams, there was a mad dash to pair up with the best students in the various different classes. Soon, a definite hierarchy developed, not unlike what many experience in school or camp when sports teams are selected.

At the very beginning, I too, endeavored to match myself with my top classmates. Fortunately, not too long into the process, I paused to reflect. I realized that the university was emphasizing teams because it had determined that teamwork was essential for success in the "real world."

Therefore, I came up with what I thought was a rather unconventional and radical idea. I would deliberately seek to pair up with a diverse set of companions. Where else would I be able to experiment with such an extraordinary array of people at a relatively low cost?

However, it was not without apprehension that I sought to pair myself with a range of teammates with whom I would never have previously thought to pair. I reasoned that due to the very large number of teams with which I would have to work over the two years, I could weather the trials of one or two more difficult teams.

Fortunately for me, it turned out to be a worthwhile and eye-opening experience for me. I learnt an extraordinary amount about myself, the people with whom I worked, and the concept of teams as a result of this "experiment." I learnt with whom I worked best and worst, how to deal with a wide range of skills and personalities, and what were for me acceptable and unacceptable team norms.

Perhaps, the most surprising and, at the same time, endearing thing I learnt was that everyone had something special about themselves. Even if an individual might be deemed "weak" by his or her peers, at some point, often to my surprise and joy, that same individual might say something brilliant, present a valuable perspective, bring much needed laughter to a stressful situation, or demonstrate a critical (previously undervalued) skill. I have since come across a quotation that probably sums up best what I learnt from that experience.

"There is an optical illusion about every person we meet." Ralph Waldo Emerson

The above statement by Emerson suggests that one's (initial) impressions of someone may not always be correct. Open yourself to meeting a wide variety of people. There may be some disappointments, but overall many will find this to be a truly enriching part of their lives.

CASE: HISTORY 1

One can find evidence of teamwork in some of the key turning point of history.

One of the important empires of history emerged from the battle of two famous ancient personalities, Octavian and Mark Antony.

Mark Antony had served as a general under Julius Caesar, the famous military conqueror who had been Rome's previous ruler, and Mark Antony essentially was Caesar's second in command. Upon Caesar's assassination, Mark Antony found himself heir to much of Caesar's wealth and prestige. Most importantly, he commanded the loyalty of the majority of Julius Caesar's legions.

Octavian, on the other hand, had a weaker claim to Caesar. He was a distant relative who, much to public surprise, was posthumously named a heir in Caesar's will (a fact upon which he later brilliantly capitalized.)

The Roman Republic had initially been divided between these individuals. Marc Anthony selected the richer eastern part of the Roman Republic while Octavian installed himself in the western part of the Republic (which included Rome). It was not long after that the two sides began to fight each other earnestly.

After a series of battles, including the decisive naval battle of Actium in 31 BCE, Octavian emerged victorious and conquered the eastern half of the Roman lands and reunited the territories. While the reasons for Octavian's victory are varied, one of the important reasons for his success was his astute use of teamwork.

While Octavian had mastered the critical art of contemporary Roman political skills, he was smart enough to recognize that he lacked vital military skills. He managed this weakness by associating himself with someone who filled this void, Marcus Agrippa. Fortunately, for him, Agrippa was more than content to handle military matters and leave the politics to Octavian. This potent combination of talent was one of the important factors that helped Octavian defeat Mark Antony. Octavian then went on to become the first emperor (Emperor Augustus) of the mighty Roman Empire.

BONUS POINTS:

On the other side of the world, in the not too distant past from Octavian, Lui Bang was born in China. He too illustrates the value of having a team.

Liu Bang was born around 256 BCE or 247 BCE. Starting from humble beginnings, he skyrocketed to success. From an illiterate peasant, he went on to found the influential Han dynasty of China and became its first emperor. Interestingly, he lost every war (except one) that he personally commanded. However, he excelled in "people skills." He adroitly mediated internal disputes, crafted alliances, and skillfully selected able subordinates. Those abilities, it turned out, were a critical set of skills.

CASE: HISTORY 2

Greece against Persia.

Just to clarify, Persia in those days was enormous–far

larger than modern day Iran. For example, in addition to Iran, it encompassed lands stretching a little beyond Anatolia (e.g., Turkey) in the west and towards the Indus river (e.g., Pakistan) in the east. It also included Egypt in the south and it was the superpower of its age.

In the other corner of the battle, were the constantly feuding small city-states of ancient Greece that were engaged in bloody and internecine warfare.

Against this backdrop, the odds seemed stacked against the Greeks when Persia began her campaigns against Greece. However, the Persian invasions served as a catalyst towards uniting the Greeks and mending them together militarily. As such, they were eventually able to transform themselves into a formidable fighting machine.

In the series of battles that ensued, things began badly for the Persians who suffered a temporary setback with their defeat at the Battle of Marathon (490 BCE) at the hand of the Athenians. However, this was followed by a subsequent Persian invasion under Xerxes I with a much larger force. Xerxes' invading army engaged in the Battle of Thermopylae, which (despite Spartan heroism) was a Persian victory, and followed it up by entering and proceeding to burn Athens to the ground. The Greeks managed to counter with an important victory at the Battle of Salamis where a significant portion of the Persian navy was destroyed.

However, things were far from settled, since a large, well trained, and powerful Persian military land force still occupied the center of Greece, and the independence of the Greeks still remained uncertain. It was at the Battle of Plataea (479 BCE) that the war between the Greeks and Persians was finally decided. The Greeks fielded the largest gathering of hoplites (heavily armed Greek foot soldiers) seen at that time—vividly displaying the obvious benefit of Greek unity. Thirty-one Greek city states stood together in their attack against their Persian enemy.

Together, the Greek city states achieved what may not have been possible for themselves individually – they won, and they won big. The Persian force was decisively defeated and their commander Mardonius was killed. The Persian superpower incursion was finally over, and the course of history changed.

THE POWER OF UNITY AND TEAMWORK.

CASE: NATURE 1

There are even examples in nature of animals "teaming up" to increase their odds of survival. One such example is the emperor penguins of Antarctica. In one of the most amazing journeys in the natural world, these penguins converge on Antarctica once a year to breed.[5] While the extraordinarily harsh natural conditions of this continent serves to protect their potential offspring from most predators, survival under extreme natural conditions is itself a challenging endeavor for the arriving penguins.

As temperatures fall during this period, winds combine to form terrible conditions for the animals. In order to survive, an amazing pattern of teamwork

---

5   See the movie classic "March of the Penguins"

emerges. The animals huddle together in large numbers to preserve their body warmth, but the plummeting temperatures and bitter winds eventually begin to wreak havoc on the penguins in the outer edge of the huddle.

Then an amazing, slow moving, and well-choreographed "dance" takes over the huddle. This "dance" precipitates a penguin flow that rotates the animals on the outer rim deeper into the huddle, while penguins in the center spiral out towards the edges. Without this action, penguins in the center would overheat, while those on the outside would freeze.

This coordinated, sharing and rationing of body heat allows all the penguins to survive the extreme weather conditions. Together, they are able to face the extreme cold.

Case: Nature 2

One obvious example of teamwork in the animal kingdom is ants. Few animals have amplified their odds of success more by working together then have these tiny animals. Ants have been seen taking down animals much larger than themselves by ganging up on them. By working together, they can also carry much larger prey.

Large ant colonies also allow for specialization, in things like reproduction, protection, and food production and collection. Ants have even been found engaging in surprising activities like farming! Yes, some South American "leafcutter" ants "cultivate" fungus for their needs. Other ants "milk" their equivalent of cows (e.g., aphids) for a sugary honeydew that they consume. These aphids are herded and protected by the ants.

Nor is teamwork simply confined to smaller animals. Even at the top of the food pyramid, one finds evidence of teamwork. For example, while lionesses are able to kill prey on their own, they choose to hunt in packs. It allows them to adopt tactics like using "herders" to drive prey towards a waiting lioness who will make the actual kill. It also allows them to take down larger prey like buffalo and younger elephants. Thus, the whole pride benefits from combining their efforts.

ANTI-CASE

Let us explore some examples of the "opposite" of teamwork.

CASE – FALL OF INDIA TO THE BRITISH

One example might be the British entry, conquest, and consolidation of power in the Indian subcontinent. One of the very early encounters (1757) finds Mir Jafar, the commander of the Nawab (e.g., ruler) of Bengal's army betraying the Nawab and allowing the numerically inferior British to establish a presence in India. India had been fragmenting rapidly after the death of Mughal Emperor Aurangzeb in 1707, and it was in turmoil. In fact, by 1739, Delhi had been sacked and the Mughal Emperor Muhammad Shah defeated by Emperor Nadir Shah (of Persia). In 1761, an epic clash between the Durrani Empire of Ahmad Shah Abdali and the Maratha Empire resulted in a huge number of casualties and in one of the largest battles of the 18th century. Into this highly divided scene, the

British inserted themselves.

British diplomacy adroitly built alliances, exploited differences, and played off rivalries to establish and consolidate British rule in colonial India. The British use of alliances was so masterful that a huge chuck of the land under British India belonged to rival Indian princes, and large numbers of Indians served under British officers. An official count of the princely states in 1947 (i.e., when the British left) was 565.[6]

British success was greatly aided by going up against a highly fragmented and divided opposition.

Case – World War II – Hitler's Huge blunder

Looking at the mindset of alliance building versus going it alone.

An example of completely ignoring teams and of going it alone is Hitler's[7] betrayal of Stalin and the ensuing disastrous German invasion of Russia.

Despite an initial alliance that between Germany and Russia that resulted in the division of Poland at the onset of WWII, the Hitler-Stalin alliance was short lived. In one of the worst military blunders in history, Hitler betrayed Stalin and invaded Russia in 1941. His surprise decision played an important role in the collapse of the Third Reich, which then ended up fighting a war on multiple fronts.

---

6   Many were small and "outsourced" many governmental matters to the British.

7   Like the average person I am no fan of war and consider Hitler an evil person—a sorry excuse for a human being. However, the purpose of this book is to illustrate certain concepts. Thus, a variety of individuals and situations are portrayed in this book without necessarily attaching a value judgement to them. The focus is instead on the particular points being discussed.

Thus, the flip side of teamwork is not to split oneself into pieces trying to "battle" too many things at once.

Okay, that's enough of that, and we're on to lighter subjects ...

FABLE/CONCLUSION

Then there is this well-known old fable[8].

Once people were shown a glimpse of Hell. It was filled with people with very long, stick-like arms. When food would be brought in, they would struggle to balance the food on their hands, then stare in agony at the delicious meal, as they were unable to bend their stiff arms to bring the food to their lips.

Next, people were shown a glimpse of Heaven. These people also had long stick-like arms, but they were beaming with happiness and enjoying themselves thoroughly. Whenever food was presented, they simply used their rigid arms to feed each other. In this way, they were all fed!

The beauty of teams.

EXERCISE #1 (STRETCH GOAL/DREAM TEAM)

Have some fun with this. What if you wanted to solve world hunger or some similar overarching goal about which you care? What dream team would you assemble? What kind of diversity would be important? What key attributes would your team have? Bonus: If you really want to have some fun, try including char-

---

8   The source of this fable is obscure. It has variously been attributed to Jewish, Chinese, Christian, Hindu, medieval European, and other sources. Also there are versions of the fable that include the feeding utensils being long (e.g., long chopsticks, long spoons, etc.) instead of long, fixed arms.

acters from fiction or even historical personalities as your teammates. Share this exercise with friends, too. See what they come up with. Compare notes. Learn from each other.

The purpose of this exercise is three-fold: 1) train your mind to think in terms of assembling teams as a way to solve problems, 2) learn to brainstorm without constraints, and 3) have fun.

EXERCISE #2 (MORE IMMEDIATE GOAL)

If you wanted to turn one of your hobbies or interests into a business startup, what team would you assemble? What kind of diversity would be important? What key attributes would your team have?

The purpose of this exercise is two-fold: 1) train your mind to think in terms of assembling teams as a way to solve problems, and 2) analyze and identify important, existing resource constraints.

SUMMARY

- Teams can beat non-teams
- Teams prevent "group think"
- Teams help prevent major errors and blindspots from occurring
- Fragmented groups can be brought together by creating a "common foe"
- Teams can be a very potent force if used properly, which is a super-ingredient for success.
- Everyone has something to offer

Chapter 5
Gratitude, Optimism, and Adaptability

"People do not seem to realize that their opinion of the world is also a confession of character." Ralph Waldo Emerson

Easiest way to be rich in life?

Be grateful. Even rich people can become easily dissatisfied if they are constantly chasing further riches. In those cases one can never be rich enough. The truth is that when you start appreciating what you have, you will begin to realize that you are much wealthier than you thought. Almost everyone can find some things about which to be grateful.

"The best things in life are free" -common saying

"Wealth does not mean, having a great amount of property, but wealth is self-contentment." Muslim saying

If you are worried about having lost a leg, consider the person who has lost two legs.

"Look at those who stand at a lower level than you, but don't look at those who stand at a higher level, for this would make the favors (conferred upon you by God) insignificant (in your eyes)." Muslim saying

One of the interesting and, perhaps, surprising things about being really grateful is that the more grateful one is, the more one appears to "receive" in many cases.

It's never too early to realize what a lot of wonderful gifts surround us during the course of our lives.

OPTIMISM

People are always looking for ways to convert lead into gold. Take two plus two and get eight. Here is an easy way for being happy: be optimistic. Smile!

As the common question goes, "Is the glass half full or half empty?". Optimists say a resounding, "Half full."

Here is a formula for happiness that takes two plus two and gives you more than four.

> "Smile, and the whole world smiles with you. Frown, and you frown alone." – common saying

ADAPTABILITY

Trivia: How adaptable are humans "hard wired" to be?

Did you know that humans are so inherently adaptable that we can be "rewired" to even "see" with our tongues? There apparently currently exists a device that takes images from a video camera and translates them into gentle, electrical impulses for a plastic "lollipop." The brains of blind people then can learn to interpret the tongue sensations and crudely "see" in many cases. The idea is inspired by the plasticity (or very high adaptability) of the brain.

Yup, pretty amazing.

Optional Section: This next part is somewhat more involved so one can skim it or skip it.

ADAPTABILITY METHODS IN A RAPIDLY CHANGING WORLD

The world is constant flux. Everything seems to be changing. Are there any ideas on handling an uncertain, ever changing, fluctuating world?

One field from which to glean insight into this problem of adaptability is technical project management. Traditionally, project management has involved planning, analysis, design, implementation, and maintenance.[1] This made particularly good sense if the problem was well defined and backed up with solid empirical data. The approach was comprehensive, and there was an attempt to fully define the problem from the onset by engaging in extensive requirements analysis.

However, what if the problem is not well-defined? Furthermore, what if the available methods of solution are themselves rapidly evolving? In short, what if the world is in rapid flux?

Many previous management techniques dealt with tasks that were predictable and repeatable. For example, Federick Taylor conducted time studies of various industrial tasks and built a data bank of time estimates for various tasks. Industries like manufacturing and construction are fields with many well-defined, repeatable tasks. In some cases, tasks even became commodified and automated over time, as humans were replaced by machines.

However, in the growth of entirely new industries, many companies found themselves embedded in un-

---

1   There are actually several ways to look at this traditionally.

certain environments with ambiguous or nonexistent data and with constantly shifting or evolving technologies.

What if your product has never existed before? In these cases, it is more important to focus on innovation than execution. In fact, one needs to create a "learning organization" to embed learning into the process of creation.[2]

One popular management framework that has emerged is called "Scrum."[3] It is a popular framework among some software startups. How does one fully define product requirements under this arrangement? Scrum does not even try. At its core, it does not pretend to fully understand, at the onset, exactly what the customer wants. Instead, it begins by "guessing" at a possible subset of the most valuable features a customer might want.[4] Most importantly, it gets immediate feedback on this pared down (but "potentially shippable") product.[5]

In a highly uncertain world, it is not at all uncommon, for the feedback to reveal important new (and perhaps radically different) preferences on the part of the potential customer. Here's the great part. Since so few resources have been committed, it is significantly

---

2   One way Scrum attempts to inspect itself is through "Sprint Retrospectives." Scrum teams are also encouraged to be self-organizing. Team owns sprint commitments to encourage teamwork.

3   In the 90's, the Scrum process was conceived by Jeff Sutherland and Ken Schwaber.

4   Actually a prioritized "Product Backlog" is created by the "product owner". Here, I am also alluding to a related concept called "MVP"(minimum viable product) popular in the "lean startup" methodology.

5   Feedback from from various stakeholders at the "Sprint Review Meeting." Sprints are short.

easier to "pivot"[6] to a completely different direction. Thus, Scrum also can serve as a risk mitigation framework, by controlling the risk of large resource misallocations by restraining premature commitments and, instead, measuring out relevant resources over time in response to changing demands.

Another important Scrum feature is that is iterates frequently. The concept of iteration is also very fundamental to the software world. For example, most software one encounters has a version number. Frequently early versions lack many features and are not as polished as later versions. In essence, one is rebuilding the same "product" over and over again[7] hopefully, getting better each time.

Thus at its core, Scrum, is empirical and iterative, and it relies heavily on early and frequent feedback. The iterative nature allows a product to change directions rapidly and evolve over time. As such, it can create very nimble and agile organizations that can adroitly chart their way through uncertain waters, gaining market share at the expense of more established, slower moving competitors.

6   Pivots (a related idea from the "lean startup movement") typically refer to the "product market fit". Products try to "pivot" until they can achieve "product market" fit, before they attempt to scale. "Growth hackers" / lean startup movement types may try to run "validated" experiments to determine how to continuously improve the product. These experiments can occur in the context of something called a build-measure-learn feedback loop. Adding these lean startup/growth hacker ideas to scrum can add more of a business component to traditional scrum (which typically is more technology focused). Some may also find the "business model canvas" / customer development process popularized by Steve Blank to be useful in this context. Note: the business iterations are not necessarily matched to the technical iterations.

7   Software versions do not necessarily correspond to scrum iterations. The scrum iteration unit is called a sprint and is usually very short. For more details on scrum, see scrum.org.

"I can't change the direction of the wind, but I can adjust my sails to always reach my destination." Jimmy Dean

EXERCISE #1

Create a gratitude journal by reflecting on one gratitude each day. For the next 30 days, list at least one thing each day for which you are grateful. Read it periodically. Smile.

SUMMARY

Gratitude, optimism, and adaptability: these are three super ingredients for successful living.

Chapter 6
A World of Dimensions

Optional Chapter: This chapter is somewhat more involved so one can skim it or skip it.

The purpose of this chapter is to learn an important skill for success: the ability to analyze problems critically. To take common complex problems, and view them through certain key filters or dimensions, and in doing so reduce the problem to its essentials, in order to glean insights.

Consider this:

What if you are a young graduate trying to decide which industry to enter?

Are there any tools to help you analyze the long-term sustainability or profitability of that industry or niche?

DIMENSIONS OF IMPORTANCE

When describing a problem it is important to decompose it down to its important dimensions. For example, Michael Porter's famous "Five Forces Model"[1] offers a way to analyze a business or industry.

He suggested five forces that could help determine the profitability of a particular industry.

His five forces are:

---

1   Traditionally, economists had constructed many economic models by assuming things like perfect information or perfect competition in an economy. Porter flipped the model assumptions and tried to image how a company might develop sustainable competitive advantage.

» barriers to market entry

» threat of product substitution

» bargaining clout of customers

» bargaining strength of suppliers

» and intensity of competitor rivalry

» *Barriers to market entry:* Ask yourself, "Would having high barriers to industry entry increase the industry's profitability?" Sure. Conversely, low barriers would decrease it as new entrants flood the market.

For example, the very high R&D costs in the pharmaceutical industry make the entry of new players difficult. Alternatively, in the news dissemination business, anyone who can point and click their way to a blog can deliver some form of news. Fewer players suggest less competition. Accordingly, the pharmaceutical industry is likely to have higher profitability.

Product substitution: If your product has many "substitutes" people can switch away from your product, reducing profitability.

Example: Consider the airline industry. If plane fares rise too much, I can choose to take the train. Thus, there is a limit to air fare hikes. High product substitution indicates potentially lower profitability.

Bargaining power of customers: Can your customers band together to demand discounts and cut into your profits? Pooling together customers as negotiating blocs increases customer power. As such, these groups can negotiate group discounts. Industries that deal with less organized customers may have higher profit margins.

Bargaining power of suppliers: Similarly how strongly can your suppliers bargain with you.

Example[2]: In the book industry, there are thousands of authors, and they are a fragmented and dispersed group. In contrast, there are very few book retailers. As such, author bargaining power is limited.

Rivalry of competitors: This also impact profits over time.

Now that you know the five forces, use them to help determine the possible profitability of an industry.

Now, let's look at a different way to cut to the heart of a problem.[3]

IDENTIFYING THE CRITICAL DIMENSION

It is important to analytically reduce something to its key dimensions. Sometimes, an existing problem will have one "super dimension," an overriding, critical dimension.

Consider Henry Ford and the automobile. Many may believe Ford invented the car. Actually, cars in many forms had been around for many years. Perhaps, he organized his company first? In fact, Ford's auto company was competing with many other companies. Perhaps he had the best car? Who is to say which company had the "best" car? In fact, there were many other great cars.

---

2   Trends and circumstances are different and can change, examples in five forces are for illustrative purposes only.
3   While Porter's Five Forces Model is very well-known, it is simply one way. A more sophisticated analysis could reveal more things.

The reason Ford "won" was simple i.e., two words: "mass manufacturing". With the Model T, Ford was able to offer a solid car at a great price to the masses. That was the overriding dimension. By winning in that dimension, he won the race.

Let's tweak our problem solving skills slightly. The following is a variation of the previous concept.

DIMENSION SELECTION

Sometimes dimensions of a problems are pre-assembled and handed to you for analysis for identifying a key dimension (dimension identification). Other times, you can engineer and craft your own dimensions by selecting a dimension (dimension selection) that allows one to *actively* shape the problem. Let us now explore this more active method of dimension selection.

Let us examine the famous "Battle of Thermopylae." When you are engaged in dimension selection, you do two things. Firstly, you seek to accentuate your strengths while protecting your weaknesses. Secondly, you force the other side to expose their weakness and idle their strengths.

Here is the chart of the two opposing forces:

Greeks:

Strengths: They had superior (hoplite) armor, highly trained Spartans, and local knowledge.

Weakness: They were outnumbered.

Persians:

Strength: They had a significant numerical advantage.

Weakness: They had weaker armor and were fighting in a foreign land.

The mechanism used to enable dimension selection was terrain. Specifically, the Greeks decided to engage the Persians at a narrow mountain pass.

This allowed the Greeks to hold off the vastly larger Persian force at the famous Battle of Thermopylae. In order to offset the significant Persian numerical advantage the Greeks cleverly choose to battle them at narrow coastal pass at Thermopalye.

This constricted passage in the mountainous areas worked to funnel the Persians along a much thinner line negating some of their numerical advantage. For example, it made it difficult for the Persian calvary to outflank the Greeks. Also many Persians soldiers were left idle since they were too far away from the Greeks to engage in battle.

The Greeks brought some of their best warriors (which included Spartans) to their front. This battle alignment forced the Persians to fight from a position of their weakness, while the Greeks fought from a position of their strength.

(The Greeks were then able to hold off the Persians until the Persians discovered a mountain path around the Greeks).

Here is another case on dimension selection:

CALIFORNIA GOLD RUSH, MINERS, AND PICKS AND SHOVELS

During the great gold rush of 1849, thousands of hopeful miners flooded California in the hopes of striking a fortune. However, as more and more miners arrived, the latter arrivals found it increasingly difficult to do well. With each new arrival, the competition only intensified. After a while, it got so competitive that a few people even started returning to the East.

Now while these late arrivals began to struggle, one group did very well. Indeed, they began to thrive. This group had chosen not to mine, but rather to cater to the ever-swelling miner population. These people were the merchants who sold the miners their picks, shovels, food, and shelter.

Moral of the story: It is important to know where your treasure is.

Well, this is enough about finding the critical dimension. How about constructing a whole new dimension!

CONSTRUCTING A CRITICAL DIMENSION

In a war, what does every general want to do? Ideally, attack the enemy without the enemy being able to strike back. Can this critical dimension of war be constructed?

Well, when the first bi-planes (precursors to modern day airplanes) were introduced, this is exactly what happened. In this newly constructed "air dimension", planes could drop bombs (or do reconnaissance) while the surprised ground troops had very few options to counter. A new dimension of engagement had been built.

EXERCISE #1

While the focus of this chapter was on business and

the military illustration of these principles, these ideas can be applied to many other realms. As such, let's have some fun by doing an exercise in a completely different realm, i.e., selecting a spouse.

Identify the most important dimensions for someone matching with you:

What three qualities (dimensions) are most important for a successful match?

Next, list two traits (dimensions) the other person cannot have.

SUMMARY

- Practice critical thinking
- Decompose a problem into its key dimensions
- Select a dimension for engagement
- Identify critical dimensions
- Construct critical dimensions

Section II: Goals

Chapter 7
Happiness: Taking Inventory

In the preceding chapters we have been discussing the skills and tools useful for extracting success. The next part deals with where we want to go in life. It is not enough to sail our boat well. We need to ask ourselves towards what direction do we want to sail our boat?

Has life been pulling you forward, without you giving much thought to where you are going?

Society has strong currents, so it is understandably easy to forget about oneself. So ask yourself: "What do YOU care about? What is important to you?" If you do not identify what is important to you, you risk letting the currents, winds, and vicissitudes of life take you where they want to go – not necessarily where might be best for you.

> "If you don't design your own life plan, chances are you'll fall into someone else's plan. And guess what they have planned for you? Not much." Jim Rohn

If you are working on someone else's dream, at least make sure that it pushes your dreams forward too.

Have you run into people that are making a lot of money, but are still secretly unhappy?

Have you achieved many things but still feel

a hollowness inside, like something is missing?

One way this can happen is when one spends too much time simply trying to pursue money and status, forgetting that money should serve a person – not vice versa?

In the words of Francis Bacon, "Money is a great servant but a bad master."

It is critically important for you to take inventory of your dreams and aspirations, what things you really care about, and what things make you happy. *Your future happiness and sense of fulfillment depend on it*!

LESS IS MORE

Let's begin easy and start with the small items first since they can add up. Thus, let's immediately hazard a quick first try at small things that might improve the quality of your life. (They do not have to be right initially.)

Activity- first try

Spend a few minutes listing some small ideas that might improve the quality of your life).

Since this is an early (optional) exercise, included below are some potential ideas that you might like (you can skim through the ideas below).

It's simply a possible list to get you started (add, substract, and edit as you wish to create your own list.)

Relationships

Do not hold grudges

Give permission for people to speak truthfully without fear of reprisals; also don't force people to side with you simply for loyalty's sake

Don't be stingy with genuine compliments

Laugh

Show moderation and balance

Set appropriate boundaries

Being self-aware and self accountable

Have good communication skills

Don't be so busy, that you forget to have kids :)

Lifestyle

Approach life with enthusiasm. After all, you only have one life to live, so you might as well live it fully. If you are going to star in the movie of your life it might as well be a movie in color, not black and white.

Develop a sense of humor – it will help you through the hard times that all people inevitably face Avoid cynical, sarcastic, or mean-spirited humor that might hurt yourself and those around you. Instead, raise your spirits and those around you, and help others laugh through a generosity of spirit.

Treat time as a precious resource

Honesty: watch out for the slippery slope that leads away from it.

Accelerate your life, do more, experience more, and do not live in your head.

Do not clutter your life with things; instead, fill your life your experiences.

It's better to be a problem solver than a complainer

Don't forget how to play and imagine

Exercise and watch your diet

Spend time with your parents

Financial

Start saving early

Distinguish between "needs" and "wants"

Take risks early in life since they are easier to recover from than those taken later

97

Acquire a good education/skillset (formally and informally). Some supplementary resources: coursera.org, edx.org, khanacademy.org, linkedin.com/learning, udemy.com thegreatcourses.com, youtube.com, and/or udacity.com. Or simply use your favorite search engine online to look for ideas.

It's a fairly long list. Did any of these items resonate with you? Would you add them to your list of things useful for a happier life?

Life requires reflection and planning, and it can take a few tries to get it right. Thus, it is never too early to build a base of ideas and skills for success.

EXERCISE #2

Now one can be doing a lot of things right. However, if one is taking six steps back for every one forward, one can quickly get into trouble. Therefore, it is equally critically important to be aware of life's pitfalls.

There are also some potentially really destructive things in life. They have the possibility of dramatically impacting your life for the worse. Life has its traps – don't find yourself impaled by one of these. (If you think this makes sense, then do this exercise, or else skip to the next section.)

List some things that should be aggressively avoided in life.

Here are some common ideas if you need something to trigger your thoughts: addiction to drugs, alcohol, gambling or smoking; extramarital activity; and crime or excessive debt.

Some may say, "Why are you including something so obvious?" Just because a pitfall is obvious does not mean it can be easily avoided, *and sometimes avoiding things is just as important as doing things.*

While these items probably do not apply to you, they may apply to a relative or friend or simply someone you know or with whom you have to deal. As such, it is good not to completely ignore them.

TACTICAL TO STRATEGIC

So far, we have been discussing some of the more tactical moves; let's now look at the bigger more strategic picture. When doing an inventory of one's life in search of happiness, there are some obvious important places to look, e.g., job, friends, and marriage for example. Here are some ideas.

JOB

"Choose a job you love, and you will never have to work a day in your life." Confucius

When you are going through life, don't just look at the dollar figures when choosing a job. Also look at how much *growth* you will get for being in the job. You may find that maximizing growth over time, may work out better for you in the long run. For example, a career is more important than a single job.

Whatever you choose to do, endeavor to do it well.

HUMAN RELATIONS

Get a friend. Your life may depend on it!

Human relations are important–perhaps even vital. For example, a landmark, longitudinal study (American Journal of Epidemiology, 1979[1]) found that connected people who socialized or volunteered were twice as likely to live longer than those who lead solitary lives.

Not only can you increase your longevity, but you can increase your happiness, too. An important, extended longitudinal study (Harvard Grant Study[2]) found that having strong social connections and relationships was *one of the strongest predictors of satisfaction in life.*

Get friends and cherish them. They are essential for your well-being.

What is a friend? (Here are some nice quotations that I found)

"Friends... they cherish one another's hopes. They are kind to one another's dreams." Henry David Thoreau

"At times our own light goes out and is rekindled by a spark from another person. Each one of us has cause to think with deep gratitude of those who have lighted the flame within us." Albert Schweitzer

"It is one of the blessings of old friends that you can afford to be stupid with them." Ralph Waldo Emerson

Yup. Friends – no matter how stupid you are with them, they, for whatever ridiculous reason, still seem to support you. It's quite incredible if you think about it.

---

1   Social networks, host resistance, and mortality: A nine-year follow-up study of Alameda. County residents. Lisa F. Berkrnan and 5. Leonard Syme.

2   75-year longitudinal study of 268 Harvard college students from the classes of 1939–1944.

If you want to acquire and keep a good circle of friends, keep these two, tiny tidbits of advice in mind:

"What I regret most in my life are failures of kindness." George Saunders

"I've learned that people will forget what you said, people will forget what you did, but people will never forget how you made them feel." Maya Angelou

MARRIAGE: SPOUSE = 90% HAPPINESS (OR MISERY)

Of course, ideally your spouse is also one of your best friends.

Some say that your spouse can be the source of 90% of your happiness (or misery). Yet, many spend more time planning and developing their careers than in matching with a suitable spouse. *Make sure you allocate enough time to find a spouse.*[3]

A marriage is not unlike bringing two notes together. They may resonate in harmony and produce a symphony, or they may be discordant and create grating, out of step sounds with each other. Strive for the former, and work to smooth out the later. There is much "give and take" in a marriage as both people adjust to each other in order to create their own unique symphony.

Humor is to a marriage like shock absorbers are to a car. Imagine driving down a rocky road with and without shock absorbers. Humor helps couples navi-

---

3   If you are interested in the "mathematics" of love check out this funny TED talk by Hannah Fry about "optimal stopping theory." https://www.ted.com/talks/hannah_fry_the_mathematics_of_love

gate the inevitable pitfalls of life with resilience.

Spend time and effort in nurturing this very important relationship. After all, a garden that is tended thrives better than one that is neglected.

SUMMING IT UP: HAPPINESS PILLARS

Here are some key ideas about happiness.

There is a lot of information, data, and research on happiness. If one pours through it, a number of common threads appear. Here are a few that I came across that appeared to be more significant:

» Having strong relationships (e.g., good friends and extended family)

» Having a good support structure

» Having a good marriage

» Your ability to turn "lemons into lemonade"[4]; to see the glass as "half full – not half empty"

» Having a good purpose in life (volunteering, interests, job, etc.)

» Being happy in your religion/spirituality (e.g., the desire to do good)

With that in mind, give yourself this important quick pop quiz.

ACTIVITY: SELF ASSESSMENT

Current Scorecard: Pillars of Happiness

Grade yourself (be honest, no one need see it but you) 1 to 5 points in each of the following

---

4   E.g., problems into solutions

important areas of happiness. (5 being best.)

Relationships (1 to 5 points), *Support Structure* (1 to 5 points), *Marriage* (1 to 5 points), *Your level of Positivity* (1 to 5 points), *Purpose* (1 to 5 points), and *Spirituality* (1 to 5 points).

Add up your points5

Total points: 0-18 points = Room for Improvement, 18-21 points = Better, 21-24 point= Good, 24-30 points= Great.

ANOTHER POP QUIZ

A person can be a member of one of three groups:

» Someone hurtling down life without even reflecting on it

» Someone nearing his/her deathbed: Alone, unhappy, confused, and uncertain whether his/her life was even lived.

» Someone living life confidently, moving in the direction of their dreams

Now look at yourself. Which way are you headed?

SCAFFOLDING TO BUILD YOUR ENTERPRISE: YOU (BONUS SECTION)

It wouldn't be very nice to get you excited about these new goals in your life without at least giving you some more encouragement in the way of some more tools to help you achieve your dreams. So here are some more ideas. Hopefully, you will like them.

In the following section, we will further augment the

---

5   This is not a scientific quiz

framework of super-ingredients explored in previous chapters – a few more bonus ideas to help you through this purposeful journey called life.

STRESS – a fable

Pretty much one of the guaranteed things in life is that you will get stressed. As such, it is important to learn how to deal with it.

In that regard, here is a story I heard a long time ago that I liked. Hopefully you too will find it helpful.

The Monarch's Ring[6]

There was once a powerful king who assembled his nobleman and asked for something that would always be true in a world of ever changing conditions.

After a long and very difficult search, he was finally presented a ring with an inscription.

When this king was at the height of his power, he looked at the ring and a tear came to his eyes.

Later when the same king was at the nadir of life, having suffered some terrible reversals, he again looked at his ring. A smile broke out over his face.

This is what the inscription on the ring said: "And this too shall pass."

He persevered and regained his glory.

So remember the phrase, "And this too shall pass" for the times you are stressed in your life. You might find that it helps.

---

6   It is an ancient fable that has various incarnations, including Muslim/Sufi and Jewish sources. The fable was also alluded to by Abraham Lincoln, a man who endured numerous difficult trials in his life, in an address in Milwaukee.

Would you like to move effortlessly towards your goals and glide forward without even thinking?

Who wouldn't!

Okay. Consider this. Remember when you first learnt how to brush your teeth? It was a real chore! Additionally once you started, you kept forgetting to do it. Yet, you kept it up, and eventually it became effortless—automatic. You didn't even have to think about it; it just happened. In fact, if you skipped it, you immediately felt something was "off." What had happened? You had acquired a habit!

One way to improve one's lifestyle is by developing good habits. Among habits, exercise is a particularly good one. The reason for this is that some habits, like exercise, are in a class of habits that when they take hold, organically and naturally stimulate grow in other healthy habits.

Here are two of the most important words towards building habits: "small" and "continuous." Remember them!

Human are creatures of inertia.

"Every object at rest stays at rest. Every object in motion tends to stay in motion." – Newton's first law

Inertia is difficult to break, especially if the task seems daunting. As such, make it "quasi trivial" in the beginning. Make it "small;" make the "hump of inertia" small. The thought of a one-hour walk may not get you off the couch. However, almost anyone can do a two-minute walk.

Here is the interesting thing about your brain: most people when they start something naturally continue it. Thus, without any effort, a two-minute walk can turn into a five-minute walk.

However don't push it. Instead, harness the next brain trick because after a while we get bored and crave stimulation.

Now remember the next word, "continuous." Perhaps more important than the length of the walk is that is be done continuously. For example, commit to 30 days of two-minute walks per day. (If you have one or two bad days, you can skip those days). The important element is to continue doing it over a long period of time.

Here is the kicker: after doing things for a while at two minutes, many people will get bored of such mild exercise and will naturally and EFFORTLESSLY increase it. Only increase it slightly though – enough to release the boredom pressure somewhat, but not completely. This is because you want the boredom pressure to push you forward effortlessly again and again in the future.

Now if one reads about habits one will come across two other words: cues and rewards. Most habits take better if they have a "cue" or trigger. Therefore, set a specific time daily, for example, as your cue. Finally, give yourself a pat on the back. Give yourself small rewards to keep you interested in the activity over time.

Bonus trick #1: Peer pressure can also be harnessed. Exercise with a buddy. Urge each other on gently.

Bonus trick #2: Some people find that listening to inspirational audio while exercising sometimes helps.

Try out these ideas. Try different time lengths. Experiment. See what works for you. If you can be continuous about it (rewards help), you just might find that it works.

Note #1: Substitute "walking" with another exercise if that is more appropriate for you situation.

Note #2: Exercise is just one healthy habit for mind and body. These ideas extend to habits in general.

HABIT ECOSYSTEM

Habits have the excellent quality of building upon each other. Healthy habits can combine in ways that can make two plus two equal more than four. Over a lifetime, you want to build an "ecosystem" of healthy habits each helping and reinforcing the other. Since habits largely operate "automatically" i.e., without much thought, healthy habits will often help you move more effortlessly in the direction of your goals. It will be as if some "unseen force" is propelling you towards your goals. *Good habits are great!*

THE IMPORTANCE OF HABITS

ACTIVITY 1 AND 2:

Select a 30-day exercise plan for yourself. Start today.

Here's another good habit: reading. Set aside a small number of minutes to read every day. Use a daily cue.

Do it for 30 days.[7] Don't forget to give yourself rewards.

Activity #3

Activity background:

What if you want to break a bad habit?

Here is one possible approach.

Bad habits are not broken; it's too difficult. Instead, they are studied and replaced, which is much easier.

"Habit loops" have three important components: the cue, the routine, and the reward. The cue is the trigger that moves you into the action. Typically, this sequence results in some sort of reward for you.

Firstly, identify the cue or trigger for your bad habit. Be very specific. Make a log to find out what your trigger is. Next, find out exactly what your reward is. For example, experiment with substituting some possible rewards to help you identify the real one.

Based on your research, when your trigger occurs, replace your old action with a new routine and reward yourself.

This brief habit breaking introduction is largely based on some ideas popularized by Charles Duhigg. A more engaging and detailed presentation of these ideas is offered at charlesduhigg.com. Check it out.

---

7   Actually even though 30 days is used in this and other exercises the time for a habit to take averages about 66 days (it can take from 18 to 254 days). See "How are habits formed: Modelling habit formation in the real world." Phillippa Lally, Cornelia H. M. van Jaarsveld, Henry W. W. Potts and Jane Wardle. European Journal of Social Psychology.

To do

Select a minor bad habit. Study it. See if you can replace it with something better.

Are you missing out on these three early wins in life?

3 USEFUL SKILLS THAT MANY PEOPLE LACK (BUT THAT ARE FAIRLY EASY TO ACQUIRE EARLIER IN LIFE)

These three skills are:

» Public speaking.

» Negotiating (and people) skills

» Understanding Economics

If you have already checked off these points, congratulations; give yourself a pat on the back and skip forward. Otherwise try the following.

Public Speaking: Start early in life and practice. You might find a group like Toastmasters(toastmasters.org) of some use. Take a course in high school if they offer it.

Negotiating (and people skills): Pick up a book like "Getting to Yes" (Harvard Negotiation Project). Read the bestselling business classic "How to Win Friends and Influence people" and take good classes/workshops on developing important "people skills." You might find some basic knowledge of "emotional intelligence" helpful too.

Introductory Economics: Beginning course on economics (e.g. Introductory Macroeconomics, etc.) Many people find basic concepts in economics counter intuitive. Whether or not you agree with everything, there will undoubtedly be some interesting concepts to enrich your analytic toolkit. As such, it may prove useful to you by offering some new perspectives with which to analyze problems. Additionally, a surprising number of things in life revolve around simple economics.

Search online for free courses. Some websites of interest might be coursera.org, edx.org, khanacademy.org and/or udacity.com.

ACTION #4

Another important piece of "scaffolding advice" is to surround yourself with good people. Moms are instinctively aware of the importance of this point. Moms know that whether their children hang out with the "wrong crowd" or with a great set of friends can strongly affect how their children turn out.

However, here's the rub: it's even important for adults! Check out this quote from Tim Ferriss, the best-selling author:

"The best advice I ever got is: 'You're the average of the five people you associate with the most.'[8]"

So, for fun, ask yourself:

» Who are the (current) five people with whom you associate the most? List any comments about them.

» Who are the (future) five people with whom you will associate the most? List any comments about them.

---

8   Quotation usually attributed to Jim Rohn

ACTION/ACTIVITY

A lot about life involves rationing. We simply don't have enough time and energy to do everything we want to. Do you have any ideas on this topic? Here's one idea.

The "Pareto Principle" or the 80/20 rule, named after Italian economist Vilfredo Pareto, suggests that 20% of task/causes will result in 80% of the outcome/effects. There are many variations of this saying. For example, the top 20% of your customers will produce 80% of your profits. End users spend 80% of their time on 20% of a software products features. Or on the other end, 20% of your customers will produce 80% of the complaints.

You could try an experiment and see if 80% of your happiness comes from ... or 20% of ... causes 80% of your distress. For some people, it might be a source of insights.

TO DO

Make a list of the top 20% of "things" that are contributing to 80% of your happiness. Now, flip it. List the top 20% of "things" that are contributing to 80% of your unhappiness. Learn anything?

Bonus: Build separate lists for long-term and short-term happiness.

CONCLUSION

Don't be the person who is lying on his/her death bed wondering if he/she lived their life properly. It's a lit-

111

tle late then. Instead, review things periodically. Ask yourself if your ship is sailing in the direction you want it to go, not necessarily where the winds are talking it.

Purposefully create your life. Life can be tricky because you are both the "sculptor and sculpture" – but it can turn out to be really wonderful!

Aim for the following:

> "You know you're in love when you can't fall asleep because reality is finally better than your dreams." Dr. Seuss

Be in love with the life you create for yourself.

SUMMARY

- Do a life inventory
- Smile. Be positive.
- Exercise, and watch your diet
- Start early saving for retirement
- Acquire formal and informal knowledge in life (also see udacity, edx, khanacademy, lynda, udemy, coursera, thegreatcourses, and/or youtube. Or simply use your favorite search engine online to search for ideas.)
- Learn early in life: public speaking, negotiating, and some economics.
- Avoid: Addiction to drugs, alcohol, gambling, and smoking, extramarital activity, crime, and excessive debt
- Seek: good friends, a good marriage, and a support network. Work on turning "lemons into lemon-

ade," as the saying goes. Give your life a purpose and joy, and enjoy your spirituality.

- Control Stress
- Build good habits
- Check out "How to Win Friends and Influence People"
- Use the 80/20 rule to help make some decisions in life

Chapter 8
Value

"Though we travel the world over to find the beautiful, we must carry it with us or we find it not." Ralph Waldo Emerson

"It is never too late to be what you might have been." George Eliot

If one reads the biographies of great people or examines major movements in human history, one finds many common threads. Prominent among these are the deep forces of justice and compassion. **Ignore these two deep wells of existence at your own great peril.** In fact, it is very difficult to talk about life without addressing these two core topics. As such, it seems only fitting that we examine them at some depth before we conclude. Indeed, they are the two main topics for this chapter.

In the first section of this chapter, we will explore empathy, one of the key wellsprings of compassion. In the second part, we will look at justice by exploring various notions of fairness

EMPATHY

"Be kind, for everyone you meet is fighting a hard battle." Philo of Alexandria

"Being deeply loved by someone gives you strength, while loving someone deeply gives you courage." Lao Tzu

What is empathy?

Empathy is understanding how similar and interconnected we are at a deeper level. It is about establishing that fundamental connection between sentient beings, and this connection can happen on several levels. First of all, there is the intellectual level, i.e., understanding from where the other person is coming and seeing things from their perspective. At a deeper level, one connects emotionally, actually feeling what the other person feels; that is deep empathy.

The importance of empathy is illustrated in the following quotation.

> "First they came for the socialists, and I did not speak out – because I was not a socialist. Then they came for the trade unionists, and I did not speak out – because I was not a trade unionist. Then they came for the Jews, and I did not speak out – because I was not a Jew. Then they came for me – and there was no one left to speak for me." -Pastor Martin Niemoller. Germany. World War II era.

Now, let us explore empathy by looking at specific intriguing cases.

> "All truth passes through three stages. First, it is ridiculed. Second, it is violently opposed. Third, it is accepted as being self-evident." Arthur Schopenhauer

USA CIVIL RIGHTS (1959)–HISTORY

John Griffin, a white Texan during the civil rights movement, took the ultimate step in empathy. He decided to take the highly unusually step of becoming "black" to temporarily experience a different world.

He began an audacious "experiment" to answer the question whether American Southerners in 1959 would treat him differently based solely on his skin color.

Using medicines, dyes, and light, he worked with a dermatologist to darken his skin artificially. He would be exactly the same person, maintaining his clothes, skills, and name. He would answer questions truthfully. The only thing that would be different as he journeyed across the Deep South would be his skin color.

His experience, chronicled in a book "Black Like Me," vividly demonstrates that one change alone (i.e., darkening his skin) was enough to dramatically change his life. It offers insight into a completely different world in a way that no academic paper or statistic could.

The impact of his work was dramatic and exposed the ugly underbelly of racism in the South. He was featured heavily in the media. Not long after his odyssey, he was hanged in effigy in his hometown. His parents were forced to leave the U.S., and he himself was reported have been beaten with chains by the Klan and left for dead in a back road in Mississippi.

Fortunately, he survived. But his book had touched a nerve, and many people supported him. He helped many non-Blacks to see the evils of racism.[1] Through his experience, he managed to transport thousands of people to an entirely different world and to experience with him the ugliness of racism.

---

1   See http://www.ted.com/talks/chimamanda_adichie_the_danger_of_a_single_story?language=en. While one cannot comment on any side issues, the core message indicating the need to see multi-dimensional characters instead of caricatures is well-presented.

Not all acts of empathy are so dramatic.

Not everyone can take such extraordinary steps to develop empathy. However, simply expanding one's set of life experiences by things like traveling, can develop empathy. Even the simple act of aging can develop empathy as one gets exposed to more life experiences.

How deeply rooted is the quality of empathy? Is it an inherent quality of many social systems? One way to explore that notion is to examine non-human social structures. The existence of empathy and fairness in non-human social creatures may suggest that such qualities can have a value in the smooth operation and cohesion of some social systems.

BONOBO MONKEYS (BIOLOGY)

Brian Hare, primatologist at Duke University and his student, Suzy Kwetuenda, performed the following experiment.

The setup:

Two Bonobo monkeys were placed in separate cages that shared a common wall. The common wall had a door that could ONLY be opened by the first monkey. Food was placed in the first monkey's cage. Would the first monkey simply enjoy the meal? (Note: The two monkeys are strangers.)

What do you think happened next?

Despite being separated by a closed door and having no overt reason to share its food, the first monkey hesitated after starting the meal.

Ultimately, the first monkey turned around and voluntarily decided to open the door and share the food with the second monkey.

Interesting, huh?

However, that is Bonobo monkeys. How about other animals? Let's look at something radically different: rats.

RATS (BIOLOGY)

Rats and Empathy? You decide.

Judy: "Do rats have empathy?"

Sam: "What?"

Judy: "Peggy Mason, a neuroscientist at the University of Chicago, ran some interesting experiments on rats. Here was the experiment. A rat was trapped in a glass tube with a closed door. The door could only be sprung from the outside. A second (free) rat was introduced to this setup. What happened?

Sam: "You're the one telling the story..."

Judy: "Well, guess what? Even though the free rat had no idea how to release the trapped rat, it repeatedly tried to rescue the trapped rat."

Sam: "Interesting. I guess it was concerned."

Judy: "Yup. It kept trying until it succeeded, in releasing the door."

Sam: "I guess it was a special rat."

Judy: "No. This experiment has been run with many different rats, and with similar results."

Sam: "Who knew? Rats, eh?"

Judy: "Wait. It gets more interesting. Mason then reran the experiment, adding an additional complication and dilemma for the free rat. This time, a second tube with food was introduced to the scenario. Would the free rat still work to free the trapped rat when it could instead have all the food to itself?"

Sam: "At this point, if I am the trapped rat, I am thinking let the food be zucchini, not aromatic, succulent cheese else I am doomed."

Judy: (laughing) "Well the free rat still worked to release the trapped rat."

Sam: "And the food?"

Judy: "The food was shared. On average, it took 3 ½ of the five pieces and left the remainder for the other rat."

Sam: "Does all this mean I have to be nicer to you?"

EMPATHY CONCLUSION

It has been said that before judging someone too harshly, try to walk in their shoes and see the world through their eyes and past experiences. People may appear "stupid," but in their internal world, built on past history, information, environment, and circumstances, their actions may in fact be logical and internally consistent. Find out what their story is before you judge them.

Besides, no one wants his/her epithet to read that they had less empathy than a rat. Make use of the wonderful gift of life.

"Love is that condition in which the happiness of another

person is essential to your own." Robert A. Heinlein

"It is one of the beautiful compensations in this life that no one can sincerely try to help another without helping himself." Ralph Waldo Emerson

Our very short exploration of empathy would not be complete without also touching on divergences from empathy.

ANTI-CASE

Let us explore an "anti-case", or the flip side of empathy, and explore the idea of "in-groups" and it's opposite "outgroups".

The Robber's Cave Experiment (1954, Muzafer Sherif) is a social psychology experiment dealing with intergroup conflict.

This classic study dealt with issues like friction between members of an in-group and an out-group. The three-week experiment was conducted in a camp like setting with 22 eleven to twelve-year old boys who did not previously know each other. It had three phases.

In the first phase, the boys were randomly split into two groups. The two groups were separated and did not know about each other. The groups then engaged in a number of team building and bonding exercises. Thus, the first phase built team cohesion and identification. This was the "in-group" phase in which the boys began to identify with their own group.

The second phase, a friction or competition phase, pitted the two teams against each other for limited resources. As this phase evolved, tension built. There was a lot of name calling, and derogatory songs were sung about other side, i.e., the "out-group". Soon, the two groups even objected to sitting together in the same room.

So this experiment demonstrates how easily empathy between humans can be severed and how fragile the natural links between humans can be.

However, don't despair. The experiment did end on an up-note. The third phase explored ways to re-establish empathy after it has been severed.

How do you think it was done?

The third phase, an integration or "coming together" stage, used superordinate goals and resource sharing to help reconcile the two groups. A common "enemy"[2] was created for the two groups. The two groups had to cooperate in order to triumph over the problem at hand. Each group was unable to solve the problem on its own. In one scenario, water stopped coming to the camp. As the boys grew increasingly thirsty, they together identified and solved the water problem, which was a blocked outlet faucet. They then shared the water. By the end of phase three, the two groups had reconciled enough to want to return to Oklahoma City together in one bus.

Interesting... huh?

Now let's look at that second, all-important concept: justice.

JUSTICE:

<u>Why is justice</u> such a widespread concept? Perhaps

2   The "enemy" can be non-human, as was the case here.

because without it societies risk becoming dysfunctional. Some sense of order is necessarily to ensure the healthy maintenance of a system.

FAIRNESS CASE (PSYCHOLOGY)

How deeply is the notion of fairness wired into the human psyche? An interesting psychology experiment in economics called the "ultimate game" sheds light on this.

Here's how the ultimate game is played. The game organizer, let's call her Jane, calls forward two people, Alice and John. The two players, Alice and John, are then told the rules.

Jane offers a hundred dollars to John. John may split the money any way he wishes between himself and Alice. Alice then either accepts or rejects the division. If Alice agrees to the allocation, both can keep the money. Otherwise, the money is returned to Jane. The game is only played once.

That's the game. Now, assume John offers Alice ten dollars out of the hundred dollars. What do you think happens next?

Now, any rational analysis would suggest that Alice should accept any split that gives her money because without an agreement she gets NO money. Ten dollars is better than zero dollars. *In actuality, when this experiment was run, most "unfair" divisions were rejected.*

People did not act "rationally." The overriding emotion governing this outcome was a sense of fairness, even if the outcome was detrimental to oneself. The perception of fairness matters. Ignore this core human trait at your own peril.

Does the notion of "injustice" extend beyond humans? For that answer, let's look at a non-human species: monkeys. Like humans, monkeys have extensive social relationships.

CAPUCHIN MONKEYS.

In this experiment, a human offered a Capuchin monkey a cucumber slice in exchange for a token. The monkey readily accepted and was *satisfied* with the exchange. Next, the human turned to a second monkey and did a similar trade. However, the first monkey noticed that the second monkey received a grape (a highly prized delicacy) in exchange for the token.

Therefore, the first monkey was then quite eager to offer the token to the human in anticipation of his next reward. The first monkey did the trade (expecting a grape like the second monkey had received) but instead received a cucumber slice yet again.

On seeing his reward, the monkey's reaction was instantaneous, he *hurled* the cucumber back, now quite piqued at the *unfair* trade. What had been a perfectly fine reward was now treated as being completely unacceptable.

The actual video is quite hilarious to watch. Search for it online.

(Interestingly, similar experiments that were done with dogs, ravens, and elephants offered similar concepts of "fairness" in some animals.)

FAIRNESS CASE

Let's get back to humans. This time, let us visit third grade Iowan teacher, Jane Elliott, during the time of the Dr. Martin Luther King's civil rights movement.

During this time of social upheaval, Elliott was struggling to explain what was happening around her to her all-white class. She didn't want her talk to be a dry, academic explanation. Then Elliot hit upon a novel approach.

She divided her class into blue-eyed students, and brown-eyed students. She began by designating the blue eyes as the superior group. They received extra praise and privileges, such as an extra five minutes in recess. They were also referred to as the more intelligent group. Soon, they began performing better than the brown eyes, and becoming bossier.

The next Monday, Elliot reversed the roles anointing the brown eyes as the superior group and the blue eyes as the inferior group. While the brown eyes relished the role reversal, they did temper their actions somewhat (remembering how they had felt previously.) Eventually, the exercise ended, and the two groups reconciled. The students were then asked to write about their reflections on the experience. Needless to say, the unfairness of being the underdog was not lost on them.

While Elliot received criticism, primarily dealing with the age of the children involved, her experiment received wide coverage. She was covered on several print publications, and appeared on a wide variety of TV shows, including with "Johnny Carson." The experiment was featured in books and documentaries.

Compassion (e.g., empathy) and justice (e.g., fairness) (along with Truth) are important pillars in a system of ethics or values. Whatever one's values are, it is important to reflect on them periodically. It is a way humans try to extract meaning from the world around them. It is what makes us who we are. It is an important source of our sense of fulfillment and achievement. It would, for example, be difficult to set something as basic as meaningful personal goals without spending some time thinking what we really care about.

TIME/VALUES EXERCISE

Someone once said that God taking away things is His way of teaching us the price of things. Often, we do not value things until we lose them. We may undervalue things we have and sometimes overvalue things we think we want. It is probably no accident that the word "values" uses the word "value," implicitly indicating the value one places on different things.

It can be beneficial to take time from our overworked schedules to take an inventory, and to reflect on where we are and where we are going. In order to create a baseline, begin by creating a diary that indicates which things you value the most by how much time you are devoting to each thing.

Use this insight: time is a currency and a very valuable one. See how you are allocating it currently on a daily, monthly, and annual basis. Next, project this exercise

10, 20, and 30 years into the future. Finally, conclude by asking yourself a few questions (remembering that time is a currency):

What was overpriced in life?

What in the long run is most underpriced?

Where did you put in too much time?

Are you setting yourself up for regrets later in your life?

Is your time tracking aligning with your values?

Sometimes, the simple act of running this exercise, and seeing how you are actually "voting" with your time for each of your values, will stir you into planning better for the long term.

CONCLUSION

We live in exciting times. The pace of technological innovation is breath-taking, exhilarating, and accelerating. Possibilities for solutions to problems that have plagued humanity like hunger and disease are so tantalizingly close. What a time to be alive! However, we cannot forget the darker side to humanity: man's inhumanity to man. Be aware of both the potential and the pitfalls!

SEIZE THE DAY

"Many men go fishing all of their lives without knowing that it is not fish they are after." Henry David Thoreau

Within this maze of possibilities, one must navigate a path. Whatever path one chooses, *enjoy the journey*, and be on the lookout for serendipity.

Sure, there are numerous challenges for humanity, but it is the most wonderful time to be alive – for the simple reason you are alive now. Thus as the saying goes "seize the day."

Complacency

Be wary of becoming complacent. Whatever you do, don't be complacent; it is the surest way of letting yourself down.

"Living is easy with eyes closed" John Lennon

"Be your own change"; do not assume others will do something.

PSYCHOLOGY BYSTANDER EXPERIMENT

There is an interesting experiment in social psychology called the "bystander effect." Basically this experiment suggests that the more people there are who are bystanders to an incident requiring intervention, the less likely a reaction is.

In one incarnation of the experiment, some smoke was introduced to rooms under two different conditions. One was where the subject was alone, and another was where the subject was in a group setting.

Which setting do you think had the slower response time?

The response time of the group setting is significantly slower than the single person setting in the experiment.

Several explanations have been offered. Diffusion of responsibility, social proof, and group cohesiveness are some examples. Under social proof, we tend to observe other peoples' reaction to a situation. If they are not treating it like an emergency, we are less likely to also. Group cohesiveness refers to how well the members of the group know each other. If the members are complete strangers, for example, instead of good friends, they are likely to respond more slowly. Finally, diffusion of responsibility refers to the idea that, "Hey, someone else will take care of it." Of course, if everyone thinks that, then no one actually acts.

Whose Problem Is It?

"This is a story about four people named Everybody, Somebody, Anybody, and Nobody. There was an important job to be done and Everybody was sure Somebody would do it. Anybody could have done it, but Nobody did it. Somebody got angry about that, because it was Everybody's job. Everybody thought Anybody could do it but Nobody realized that Everybody wouldn't do it. It ended up that Everybody blamed Somebody when Nobody did what Anybody could have done."

Source Unknown

ACTIVITY #2

"The journey of a thousand miles begins with one step."
Lao Tzu

List the five top dreams you have for yourself.

ACTIVITY #3:

Activity Background:

Understanding perspectives: A me-centric perspective on life is so deeply ingrained that it can have subtle, unanticipated, and even surprisingly effects. As such, it can be exploited in business transactions, for example.

Let's say you want to ask your boss for a raise. Which of the two sentences below is more likely to be received positively?

1) I believe I am due for a 15% raise. During the last year, I increased sales 20%, cut defects 6%, and cut product cycle times by 10%.

2) During the last year, I increased sales 20%, cut defects 6%, and cut product cycle times by 10%. I believe I am due for a 15% raise.

Interestingly, a study in the Journal of Personality and Social Psychology[3] suggests that *leading* with the benefits as seen from the perspective of whomever you are talking to, versus the benefits as seen from your perspective, is likely to elicit more positive response even though both statements are factually identical. (Using that logic, statement #2 would be preferred over statement #1).

Thus training yourself to being able to see things from someone else's perspective (the first step towards empathy) can accrue major benefits to yourself!

To Do:

Try to use the technique just discussed in the next few negotiating situations in which you find yourself during the next 30 days.

---

3   Procedural frames in negotiations: how offering my resources versus requesting yours impacts perception, behavior, and outcomes. By Trötschel, Roman; Loschelder, David D.; Höhne, Benjamin P.; Majer, Johann M. Journal of Personality and Social Psychology, Vol 108(3), Mar 2015, 417-435.

Examples might include te following:

» husband/wife discussions

» arguments between siblings

» negotiations between team members

» trying to sell something

» trying to buy something

SUMMARY

- If you want to explore some super-ingredients towards a bright life, begin to understand the deep forces of fairness, compassion (e.g., empathy), and truth and how they relate to your place in the world.

- Periodically rank the things you really value in life

- Don't be a bystander in life; live life fully

Epilogue

A ship in harbor is safe, but that is not what ships are built for.

John Shedd[1]

It is not the critic who counts; not the man who points out how the strong man stumbles, or where the doer of deeds could have done them better. The credit belongs to the man who is actually in the arena, whose face is marred by dust and sweat and blood; who strives valiantly; who errs, who comes short again and again, because there is no effort without error and shortcoming; but who does actually strive to do the deeds; who knows the great enthusiasms, the great devotions; who spends himself in a worthy cause; who at the best knows in the end the triumph of high achievement, and who at the worst, if he fails, at least fails while daring greatly, so that his place shall never be with those cold and timid souls who neither know victory nor defeat.

Theodore Roosevelt

Congratulations on completing this book! You have had a chance to reflect on your life's goals and dreams. You are also now equipped with a better-defined tool-kit/framework to pursue the life you seek for yourself.

I would encourage you to select *two* things that spoke to you in this book. Try *immediately* incorporating them (or better, a personal variation) in a positive way into your life. *Bonus tip:* Follow this up by *com-*

---

1   Popularly attributed

mitting publicly now to these two concrete personal steps (if appropriate) before selected family (and/or friends) if you feel that this might actually strengthen your resolve.

Repeat these steps as needed. It is only by incorporating changes to your life that you can extract the maximum value from any work.

You have a great life ahead of yourself. Don't squander it. Relish it. Enjoy it. Live it fully to the best of your ability. And hopefully in the process make the world a better place.

Wishing you all the best on your journey through life!

Just to recap here are a few highlights from the book:

» Play with the following super-ingredients for success: drive, imagination, learning to understand and handle failure, teamwork, habits, gratitude, optimism and adaptability

» Take a life inventory; make sure your journey is a happy one

» Reflect on the deep wells of compassion (e.g., empathy) and fairness

- Do a life inventory
- Smile. Be positive.
- Exercise, and watch your diet
- Start early saving for retirement
- Acquire formal and informal knowledge in life (also see udacity, edx, khanacademy, lynda, udemy, and coursera, thegreatcourses, and/or youtube. Or simply use your favorite search engine online.)
- Three things to learn early in life are: public speaking, negotiating, and some economics.
- Avoid: Addiction to drugs, alcohol, gambling, and smoking, extramarital activity, crime, and excessive debt
- Seek: good friends, a good marriage, and a support network. Work on turning "lemons into lemonade," as the saying goes. Give your life a purpose and joy, and enjoy your spirituality.
- Control Stress
- Build good habits
- Read "How to Win Friends and Influence People"
- Use the 80/20 rule to help make some decisions in life.
- If you want to explore some super-ingredients towards a bright life, begin to understand the deep forces of fairness, compassion (e.g., empathy), and truth and how they relate to your place in the world.

- Periodically rank the things you really value in life
- Don't be a bystander in life; live life fully
- Drive (success super-ingredient) = (I)nitiative + (B)elief + (P)assion (P)ersistence + (R)esilience
- Trying too hard to avoid failure can sometimes lead to failure
- Failure can be a mirage
- Failure can be stepping stones
- Find success behind failure
- Create a proper mind-set
- Failure is temporary; get back up
- Persistence is important
- There can be great rewards
- Learn to manage risk
- Learning to handle failure well can became a super-ingredient for success
- Teams can beat non-teams
- Teams prevent "group think"
- Teams help prevent major errors and blindspots from occurring
- Fragmented groups can be brought together by creating a "common foe"
- Teams can be a very potent force if used properly; they can be a super-ingredient for success.
- Everyone has something to offer
- Gratitude, optimism, and adaptability are three super ingredients for successful living

- Practice critical thinking
- Learn to decompose a problem into its key dimensions, select a dimension for engagement, identify critical dimensions or construct critical dimensions

SOME LINKS

Website:

fuadakamal.com (Check out some of my other books.)

Facebook Page:

https://www.facebook.com/fuadakamalbooks/